T5-CPX-783

Chances & Choices

How Women Can Succeed in Today's Knowledge-Based Businesses

JANET C. WYLIE

EBW
Press

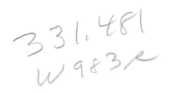

EBW Press
Vienna, VA

Publisher's Cataloging in Publication
(Prepared by Quality Books Inc.)

Wylie, Janet C.
　　Chances & choices : how women can succeed in today's
knowledge-based businesses / Janet C. Wylie.
　　p. cm.
　　Includes bibliographical references
　　ISBN 0-9649418-1-3

1. Women in business. 2. Women executives.
3. Management. 4. Corporate culture. I. Title: Chances and
choices.
HD6054.3.W95 1996　　　　　　331.4'81'6584
　　　　　　　　　　　　　　　　　95-96011

Contents

v

Foreword

As a former Secretary of Labor, and first Chair of the Glass Ceiling Commission, I have sought to identify and remove the barriers to opportunity for women and minorities in corporate America. In addition to raising the awareness levels in the corporate suite to these barriers and their effect on businesses, we examined the success factors in diverse companies and made this information available to other companies so that more and more companies can come to the view that equal opportunity for women and minorities is both smart and right as we move toward the 21st century.

Since leaving the federal government, I have had the opportunity to work with a number of private corporations. While they and others realize that change is not easy, their commitment to diversity as a bottom line issue is at the core of their future strategies. The more that companies realize the positive effects that diversity will have on their returns to their shareholders, the more progress women and minorities will experience in our nation's corporations.

In *Chances & Choices: How Women Can Succeed in Today's Knowledge-Based Businesses*, Janet Wylie addresses the business and economic environment that is providing an unprecedented opportunity for women in the work force. She goes a step further than other authors on business or diversity by advising women — practically, pragmatically, and with real life stories — on how to take charge of their careers and leverage the opportunities provided by this dynamically changing environment.

I believe that the time is right for women to take charge of their careers and realize their goals as both participants and leaders in today's global economy. Women-owned businesses are the job-creation leaders in America today. Women are making significant contributions in virtually every sector of our economy. Likewise, the time is right for corporations to address the bottom line issue of diversity and remove the barriers to success for women and minorities as they reach for their dreams. Shattering the glass ceiling may mean a messy room for a while. But in the long run, glass distorts. Having an open view of the future is going to be good for everyone who's anywhere — either looking down or looking up.

-Lynn Martin

Acknowledgments

I learned from writing and publishing this book, that a book is by no means a solo effort. There were many people who played key roles who should be acknowledged:

Tom Robinson, my boss at the time, who helped me develop the idea for the book and encouraged me to write it. He's one of the good bosses.

Sandi Walker, a friend and co-worker who gave me lots of ideas, especially about working mothers and company ownership, and contributed heavily to Chapter Fifteen.

Gus Siekierka, another co-worker who read every word and gave me valuable advice throughout the project.

Larry Pfaff, who was kind enough to take a call from a perfect stranger and share not only his assessment center data, but his ideas for marketing and distribution, as well.

Maggie Bedrosian, another brave soul who not only talks to strangers, but lends so much creativity and excitement to everything she does. Maggie had a lot of influence on my decision to self-publish and was always willing to offer advice and counsel.

Kay Supplee, a dear friend for a number of years, who faithfully read every chapter (again and again) and gave me many helpful comments and ideas, from themes to stories to titles.

Heather Rosenker, a wonderfully creative woman who opened up her network to me and helped me generate numerous marketing ideas.

Christine Bernstein, who was generous enough to share many of her stories about recruiting and starting her own business.

The friends and business associates who were generous enough with their time to read the entire manuscript and give me their reactions and comments: Bert Concklin, Mike Cook, Terry Kees, Susan Mann-Hammack, Lynn Martin, Norma Ory, and Judy Rosener.

My editor, Jean Lawrence, who not only tried to correct my errors in spelling and grammar, but tried to keep me on-track and on-message.

Stacey Anttila, who was supposed to proofread, but did so much more, and added so much value.

And then there were the many other friends and business associates who were kind enough to review chapters or make contributions in other ways: Jerry Anderson, Lyn Burchfield, Bill Farmer, Carol Fenske, Nikki Gordon, Kaz Herchold, Mike Higgins, Michelle Hupp, Mary Jo Morris, Mark Rhode, Al Risdorfer, Mark Rosenker, Lorrie Scardino, Jaimie Somers, Barbara Sweet, and Carol Walcoff.

And of course, my wonderful husband, Jim, who tip-toed around my messes for many months and ate lots of micro-meals while supporting this whole project in any way he could from beginning to end.

Thank you all.

Introduction

It's been an entire generation since the seventies, when women first started entering the work force in significant numbers. Although women have made tremendous strides toward increasing their presence in the workplace and in the salary structure, they have hardly begun to penetrate the invisible glass ceiling that separates them from the power elite of the organizations in which they work. I've spent much time wondering why this is so and researching how significant women's gains really are. During my research, it became apparent that while the gains to date are not exactly stellar, something exciting is happening in corporate America.

Corporations are changing the way they structure and manage in order to stay competitive and retain and motivate the new breed of employees — *the knowledge workers* — they now employ. Everything is changing, including the skills that are now desired in today's managers and leaders. Command-and-control is out. Coaching, facilitating, and team-building are in. What were once considered weaknesses in women's management styles are now considered strengths in the managers of the corporations of tomorrow.

This book looks at these and other changes and how they will favor women in the work force. I contend that, at last, because of the changes in our economy and business climate, it's women's turn to lead our nation's business cultures into the next century. Women have what it will take for companies to survive and thrive in the rapidly evolving information age — where knowledge is the key driver and new leadership paradigms are emerging as industries struggle to stay afloat amid waves of change.

THAT WAS THEN . . .

In the seventies, when women began demanding an equal role, they found they were entering a foreign territory for which their natural tendencies, acculturation, and training had ill-prepared them.

Command-and-control management, as defined by U.S. Army General Maxwell Taylor, was the predominant mode of operation. Although many "new" theories of management were touted — Management by Objectives, among others — these methods were employed through hierarchical structures led by managers who commanded the activities of those beneath them.

In a still expanding economy, these methods served companies and the men who led them well. Companies grew at a rate that allowed the absorption of the multi-layered infrastructures characteristic of large, successful organizations of the time. Work was delineated, with strict boundaries between specialists who performed narrowly defined tasks. Bureaucratic procedures were required to coordinate work as it passed through the many hands it took to complete the product or provide the service. Management by directive and paternalism were well-suited to the strengths and learned behaviors of the men who populated the work floor and the boardroom. And as they had in the service or on playing fields, men vied with each other for position and rank.

The barriers to women entering this territory were many and obvious. The predominantly white males over 50 who controlled most of industry believed that women belonged in the kitchen, the bedroom, or anyplace but the boardroom. There were still many social pressures on women to stay at home, raise the children, and "keep the house." Few women had the emotional support of their families to give up full-time child rearing, waxing floors, and making that perfect cup of coffee in order to pursue their careers.

The women who decided to break through the barriers of social mores and upbringing got to the workplace and found that they were pioneers, with no role models, no mentors, and many pressures. The innate skills that they possessed — to build consensus, stay out of the limelight, control indirectly — were not valued. In fact, these characteristics were viewed as weaknesses by the men who controlled the organizations in which women worked. Consensus building was seen as an inability to make decisions; modesty as incompetence;

and indirect control as manipulation. These characteristics got in the way of women's attempts to climb corporate ladders — ladders that were blocked by men who held women's styles against them. And those women who tried to change their styles — be more directive, showcase themselves, and control directly — were criticized and shunned. Caustic labels ("rhymes with rich") were attached to approaches in women that paralleled the normal behaviors of successful men.

And so, the women's movement that started so boldly and held hope for so many faltered. The idea and the message were wonderful. But the economic environment and the demographics at the time were not aligned to force businesses to affect change.

THIS IS NOW . . .

Today, more than 20 years later, the world has changed. Many companies are now run by a new generation of men — men with working mothers, working wives, and soon-to-be-working daughters who have a different view of women's roles. Even more importantly, our nation has moved from a manufacturing economy to a knowledge-based economy with global markets and diverse customers. The authoritarian style of 20 years ago is no longer effective — managers today must manage a much more diverse labor pool that is more educated, more individualistic, and intolerant of the old style of management. Successful executives today must know not only how to manage, but to *lead* this new style of worker. They must learn how to gain results through the use of teams and collaborative relationships.

Global competitiveness has forced many companies to question how they have conducted business in the past, and, indeed, to "reengineer" many of their processes and, in some cases, their entire corporations. Many companies have found that they can no longer survive under the large bureaucracies and heavy cost structures they have built over the past generation — as evidenced by massive corporate downsizing in the last five years. Every hire today must be strategic — companies can no longer add to their infrastructures without adding to their bottom line. Self-empowered teams and managers, who must act as coaches and facilitators, are required in order to compete in today's environment, yet this new breed of leader seems to be in short supply in most corporations.

Changing demographics are beginning to impact companies as well. While there was a time when corporations could pick the plums from the tops of graduating classes and staff their companies with white males, those times are over. Fifty-four percent of the undergraduate and 51% of the master's degrees now go to women. Women are represented at the tops of their classes in approximately the same proportions. Corporations that do not open their doors to recruit women must dip below the top graduates and settle for less skilled men to fill those slots. And less skilled they are. According to recent management assessments, when tested, women outscore men in nearly every category associated with management and leadership — whether rated by their bosses, employees, or themselves. These data shatter the long held belief that putting women in positions of power and leadership is "risky."

So, what should companies do? Get rid of the informal barriers that exist in many of our major companies today. Bring women in and pull them up in the ranks where their talents and skills can help their corporations get competitive and stay there. The "new" skills corporations seek in their leaders are not new to women. Women have always used them in their homes, with their families, and with their friends. Some women have even been so bold as to use them in their jobs. However, until corporations found that the old style of managing wasn't effective anymore, women's skills weren't valued. Today, the environment has changed, and women have an opportunity they have never had before to jump ahead and lead in our nation's major corporations, using the same skills they have always possessed.

Many people believe women *have* made great strides in breaking the glass ceiling and taking leadership positions in our major corporations. Yet, even with a rich feeder base of professionals developed over the past 20 years, fewer than 3% of Fortune 500 corporate officers today are women. Even more astounding, more than half of these same corporations have *no* women at the vice president level or above. Even with the women's movement of the seventies, women have made only small steps up the ladder. I believe a large part of this is due to the fact that women's skills have only recently come in phase with the unique requirements of managing knowledge workers. Now that women's skills *have* come of age, they need to combine those skills with business savvy in order to get ahead.

Even with excellent skills, *no* gender barriers and *no* discrimination, there are not many jobs at the top. The road there is fraught with numerous hazards, most of which women have not been trained or socialized to handle. Many books have been written for and about women in business. I've read dozens of them. What struck me was that they were written by psychologists, sociologists, researchers, and academics. *They were not written by women in major corporations who had experienced the culture and knew what worked and what didn't.*

What I've put together in *Chances & Choices: How Women Can Succeed in Today's Knowledge-Based Businesses*, is a guide to show women how best to use their innate skills. I address many of the hazards women will encounter in their careers. I deal with those hazards in practical ways, drawing upon my own successes and failures in corporate America, as well as those of others I've observed or interviewed. My advice is intended to support, mentor, and coach women on how to take advantage of this exciting opportunity provided by the shift in our nation's economy and the changing demographics.

Many of my reviewers asked why I targeted women for this book. They felt that good advice was good advice — for any gender. For the most part, this is true. But women face some unique challenges because of innate characteristics, socialization, and corporate culture that I wanted to address specifically. My intent was not to exclude men. In fact, I believe many men would benefit from the insight gained from understanding the challenges that the women with whom they work face. Additionally, most men can benefit from the tips and advice on managing knowledge workers and managing dynamically changing businesses. And, above all, I hope the CEOs reading this book will redouble their efforts to take maximum advantage of women's unique and useful management skills.

For all readers, I've included many vignettes and anecdotes, because I believe real-life experience is the best teacher. I've italicized the stories to make them easier to find, and I've removed the names of the people and the companies, not only to protect the innocent, but to protect the guilty as well.

The enclosed material is intended to entertain and inform. It contains a message that I feel strongly needs to be told, but it is not a cure-all for everyone's career ills. *Your experiences and career path may vary.* It is up to you to shape my advice to your unique circumstances.

Chapter One

Chances and Choices

With the shift to a knowledge-based economy, and with the changing demographics and impending labor shortage, women have an opportunity they have never had before to lead in their organizations.

The time for women to make major inroads in our nation's corporations is at hand. The economic and cultural stage is set. The drivers of the information revolution, the constricting economic environment, and the post baby boom demographics of the 1990s, create an unprecedented environment of change in the way work is performed and the way companies are managed. Women bring to this new environment the essential skills needed to assume leadership.

1

In fact, women today are forging their careers at a time that offers the best opportunity for success that women have seen for centuries.

Of course, women's ability to take advantage of this opportunity is hampered by the chances they have not been able to take in the past — chances to tackle the tough assignments and experience the failures through which leadership is learned. The one major accomplishment of affirmative action programs has been the consciousness-raising that has led many companies to at least consider a woman's request for these growth assignments. Finally, women can demand the chance to have the experiences that test their abilities and hone their leadership skills.

Given these chances, the steps women take and the choices they make will determine for each of them how far she goes and what she accomplishes. Breaking through the barriers of the past requires strong commitment and effective planning. For those who decide to take advantage of this exciting business environment through smart planning and hard work, the sky is no longer covered by glass.

CHANCES PRESENTED BY THE BUSINESS ENVIRONMENT OF THE 1990s

In the late eighteenth century to nineteenth century, the U.S. had a predominantly agrarian economy. Brute strength was needed to plow the land, plant and harvest the crops, and take the harvest to market. From the mid-1800s to about 1918, the country experienced the industrial revolution. Commodities produced in cotton and textile mills and cheap steel were shipped over burgeoning railways or on steamships. Managers, for the most part, managed uneducated and fairly unskilled workers.

By 1918, Henry Ford had invented the mass-manufactured automobile, and factories that produced other mass-manufactured goods were beginning to be a way of life in America. Machines began to replace brute strength. Access to key industrial resources and the means for transporting finished products led to the evolution of large companies located in cities close to supplies of raw materials or major transportation systems. The manufacturing process broke work down into specialized tasks performed by skilled or semi-skilled workers. The task of management was to motivate these semi-skilled people to do the same repetitive task all day long and to coordinate the assembly and distribution of the products. Strong command-and-control skills were required to keep the factories and plants running smoothly. This worked well for about 60 years. Then things began to change.

The introduction of the computer began the change from the industrial age toward the information age, or the *knowledge age*, to which we are still evolving. By 1981, the impact of this new revolution began to be felt in all facets of our economy and culture. We moved quickly through the 1980s into an economy driven by technology and information. Today, 34% of our Gross National Product comes from this *new economy* of knowledge-based businesses.

In spite of the nation's dramatic shift to an economy of *knowledge workers* (versus factory workers), the indicators we use to measure and define the health of the economy do not address the emerging economic drivers. We continue to track and measure the indicators of an industrial or manufacturing economy, such as pig iron and machine tool production or even housing starts. But the truth is, these are no longer valid indicators, as ours is no longer an industrial economy. The pig iron market is now smaller than the cookie and cracker market in the U.S. — hardly a leading predictor of our economic condition!

We cannot manage knowledge workers like we managed factory workers.

Nuala Beck, economist and author, writes in her book *Shifting Gears* of the danger of tracking a "New Economy" with old indicators. She discusses how each major economic shift has brought with it its own infrastructure, its own technological pacesetters, its own emerging industries, and its own way of organizing work. "What doesn't (and can never) work," she asserts, "is the grafting of old approaches and structures onto the New Economy."

While it is apparent that we have not yet fully grasped the impact of the information revolution, some things are becoming clear regarding the work force and its leadership. In our new economy, *knowledge* is the asset most valued. Gaining this asset and exploiting it to meet a company's goals have become serious challenges for management. More workers are highly educated. More jobs involve the transformation of information, not plastic or steel. What companies need, and this new breed of workers provides, is *knowledge* — be it in computers, accounting, law, medicine, or the multitude of other information areas now driving our economy.

Managing these skilled resources — these *knowledge workers* — is quite different. A good salary and job security do not motivate them. They know the value of their knowledge and skill and move frequently from one organization to another to find challenging, rewarding work. They want to see the whole picture, be a part of decision making, part of a team. This motivates them. Autocratic command-and-control management does not.

Just as the traditional economic indicators of the past no longer make sense, the old management practices of the industrial era do not carry over. It has become apparent in most service companies that the command-and-control skills that made manufacturing lines run smoothly do not work so well on a diverse pool of highly educated knowledge workers. These workers expect to be treated as individuals with unique value, and have their opinions heard, as well as participate in running the business. Managing this new breed of worker requires skills such as coaching and facilitating, team-building and networking. These are quite different from the factory management skills of our parents' generation. The table below highlights some of the changes in management methods and style that have resulted from the change to a knowledge-based industry.

What's "Out" With The Old Economy	Whats "In" With The New Economy
Hierarchies	Networks
Commanding	Coaching
Structure	Flexibility
Stability	Change
Empire building	Team building
Stove-pipe functional organizations	Cross-functional process teams
Directing	Facilitating
Labor as a necessary evil	Labor as a primary asset
Traditional, long-term organizational structures	Reengineered organizations
Job security	Downsizing/restructuring/ outsourcing
Annual pay raises	Pay for performance
Investments in plant and equipment	Investments in training and development
Homogeneity in the work force	Diversity

Companies are faced with a dilemma. Most top executives came up the chain using the old ways of managing. They are at a loss when it comes to managing teams instead of hierarchies and coaching instead of commanding. However, success in the new economy demands self-managed workgroups — not pyramid structures — and coaches and facilitators — not commanders. Fortunately for these companies, they have a little-recognized and often overlooked resource in their midst that can go a long way toward helping solve this management problem. *Women.*

Women have always been coaches, facilitators, and team builders. It's just now that the economy has shifted to be in phase with their skills.

Women are natural coaches, natural facilitators, and natural team builders. Centuries of balancing priorities in the home and of being the nurturer and peacemaker have taught women how to be sensitive to others' needs, how to negotiate, solve problems, and gain consensus. Women have been the "glue," often invisible, holding the home together. Even now, this carries over into the workplace, as women, often in support positions, keep things running.

THE NUMBERS GAME

During the baby boom era of the forties and fifties, single income families were the norm, most women didn't work outside the home, and the average family had 3.7 children. These children then grew up, went to college, and began very nontraditional lifestyles. The women started careers in record numbers; and couples waited to get married, waited even longer to have children (if they had them at all), and then had only 1.8 per family — not even enough to replace themselves in the work force. Now, those children have grown up, are graduating from college, and are entering the work force. *The problem is, there are not enough of them.*

Because of the low birth rates of the seventies, statistics point to a severe labor shortage starting in the mid-nineties and extending into the early 21st century. This human resource shortfall will coincide with a time of economic expansion and technological change, making businesses' needs for highly skilled workers even harder to fill. Who will do the work in the 21st century?

This question was answered recently by the management consulting and accounting firm, Deloitte & Touche: "No business can afford to waste the experience and talent of half the world's population. For Deloitte & Touche, the 'business imperative' is our need to attract, develop, encourage, and retain intelligent and highly skilled women."

With the impending labor shortage, companies that wish to grow cannot afford to ignore women as a resource.

In addition to being alarmed by the labor statistics, Deloitte & Touche was also concerned by the fact that the women they did have were leaving the company in numbers much higher than the attrition numbers for men — 25% versus 15%. In essence, the investments they had made in recruiting and training women were walking out the door. They took action. The company set up a formal "Initiative for the Advancement of Women." They established a task force to study the issues and determine why women were leaving the company in such large numbers. What they found was revealing. There were three main reasons women left. *Notice that pay and children are not on the list.*

- The environment in which the firm operates
- Perceived obstacles to career advancement
- Balancing multiple commitments in professional and personal lives

To further understand the issue of balancing multiple commitments, the firm conducted a work/life survey to find out what employees thought was important in a work environment. They found that balance was not a *women's* issue. Both men and women at every level shared this concern. Flexibility and schedule control were important to every employee.

7

Deloitte & Touche decided to do something about their findings. The firm appointed a senior partner, Ellen Gabriel, to be "National Director for the Advancement of Women." They instituted training programs for all managers and partners. And they instituted more flexible working policies. They have made measurable progress. Attrition for women is down to 15%, the same as for men. I asked one female partner if she really noticed a difference and she said, "Yes. A few years ago the women, even if they were clearly the best for the job, were less frequently considered for assignments that called for lots of travel away from home, especially if the women had children. Now at least the men know to ask, and often when they do, they are surprised to find that the women are interested in the same opportunities the men are."

Women have pushed for more flexible work environments, but all employees have benefited from this increased flexibility.

With respect to more job flexibility, what began as a women's initiative has had positive impact on male employees as well. One male audit manager found that after seven-day work weeks and years of heavy travel, he had hit the wall. In desperation, he told his boss he had to find something else to do. Much to his surprise, he was offered an 80% work schedule, a compromise that allowed him to stay with the firm.

Other, more visible men have been in the press as a result of their desire to balance their work and home lives. Jack Pope, former United Airlines president, decided not to re-enter the job market because he was tired of "being a C+ in all the outside things I do." Another example was the suit against financier Ronald Perelman filed by his former CFO, Fred Tepperman. Tepperman claimed he was fired because he refused to shun his daily obligations to his wife, who is stricken with Alzheimer's disease.

Deloitte & Touche and many other successful companies have finally discovered that factoring women and the issues they bring to the table into a company's human resource and hiring strategies is just good sense. Women today account for nearly 50% of all full-time workers and 54% of college graduates. Not only can companies no longer afford to squander this large talent base, but they are also finding that all employees benefit from the issues of consideration and flexibility women raise in the workplace.

Diversity has a positive impact on a company's bottom line. What company can afford not to support it?

IT'S GOOD BUSINESS

A 1993 study by Covenant Investment Management showed that women impact more than the human resources side of companies. They have significant impact on the bottom line. **Companies that rated in the bottom 100 on glass ceiling related measures earned an average 7.9% return on investment (ROI), compared to an average return of 18.3% for the top 100 most diverse companies. This flowed through to the stock price as well. Companies with strong Equal Employment Opportunity (EEO) compliance outperformed the Standard and Poor's 500 stock market average by 2.4% per year over a five-year period. On the other hand, companies with poor EEO compliance underperformed by 8% per year.**

Why? Women and minorities represent a strong customer base for most companies, especially in the area of consumables. Diverse companies produce products and services and the associated marketing programs that appeal to a wider consumer base — thereby increasing their revenues, profits, and corporate value.

Given that a company's willingness to employ a diverse work force can cause as much as a *10% per year* swing in their ROI, as well as their stock price, executives should treat diversity as a bottom line business issue, as Deloitte and Touche has, not as a legal or equity issue.

James Champy, author of *Reengineering Management*, sums it up well, "No manager can afford a homogeneous work force. Not only is imposing one against the law, not only is finding one an impossibility in most communities, not only does encouraging one contradict most companies' values, homogeneity is extremely bad for business. Racial, religious, ethnic, gender diversity, on the other hand, is demonstrably good for business. . . . We need different perspectives to solve the problems of the new work. Diversity of viewpoint creates the best solutions."

The Glass Ceiling Commission, a bipartisan organization commissioned by President Bush and congressional leaders in 1991, detailed in their 1995 report what makes corporate diversity successful:

- Has CEO support
- Is part of the strategic business plan
- Is specific to the organization
- Is inclusive — does not exclude white men
- Addresses preconceptions and stereotypes
- Emphasizes and requires accountability up and down the line
- Tracks progress
- Is comprehensive

Corporations concerned about return to shareholders should take note of the data provided by Covenant, Deloitte & Touche, Champy, and the Glass Ceiling Commission, and should question whether they have done all they can to leverage their resources and maximize their return. It's important to note that the success of any diversity program is its inclusivity — including majority males. Teamwork is what it's all about — maximizing everyone's productivity and excluding no one.

CHANCES WOMEN HAVEN'T HAD

For the most part, women in major corporations in America have not had the same chances men have. There are many reasons for this. Most are rooted in outdated ideas about what women can do and what they want to do. The perception still exists among the men who run corporations that women are not as intellectually competent, won't make the commitment needed, won't travel or work long hours, and won't make tough decisions. Many are still reluctant to put women in key positions because they will "get pregnant and leave."

A recent survey by Hendrick and Struggles shows that less than half of career-oriented women are choosing to have children. If companies make the assumption that a woman they hire will have a child while in their employ, they will be wrong more than they will be right.

The last two decades of data have proven that these are myths. Women are not only more than half of the total graduates, they make up one-third to one-half of the graduates in many of the top professions (accounting, engineering, law) and are well-represented at the tops of their classes. These women go to work and work just as hard and just as long as the men. They make just as many tough decisions. And though it is obviously true that the women are the ones having the babies, the vast majority of them come back to work with little interruption after the initial six-week absence.

Let's put this in perspective. Six weeks is the same amount of time that most Europeans get for vacation annually, and is roughly equivalent to the amount of time most middle-aged men who have heart attacks or drug or alcohol problems need to recuperate before they return to work. Viewed in this manner, the possibility of a short-term leave hardly seems like a valid reason to deny opportunity to 51% of the population. Especially when the possibility is becoming

11

more and more remote. A recent survey by Heidrick and Struggles, an executive recruiting firm, shows that less than half of career-oriented women are choosing to have children. If companies make the assumption that a woman they hire will have a child while in their employ, they will be wrong more than they will be right.

Another key reason that women don't get the same chances as their male counterparts has to do with the discomfort many men have working with women. Men are not as comfortable with women as they are with other men. As Deborah Tannen describes in her book, *Talking Nine to Five*, men have well-developed methods of communication with each other. They know what they mean when they speak, and they know what to expect from each other. They aren't always so sure of these things when they are dealing with women. Thus, when it comes to selecting a person to fill a key role or address a high-risk situation, they naturally (and often unconsciously) select another man.

Given the choice, most men would still prefer to work in all-male environments. They must have a compelling reason to think or act differently.

In her book *America's Competitive Secret: Utilizing Women as a Management Strategy*, Dr. Judy B. Rosener tells us that many male executives would still prefer an all-white male environment, if their companies, their clients, and their governments would let them. She goes on to discuss how many men feel "a loss of control, a blurring of self-image, and an increase in sexual static" when they are forced to compete with women in the workplace. Some women have worsened this situation inadvertently by not setting clear boundaries for what they consider acceptable behavior by their male counterparts. As a result, many men feel confused about what they can and cannot say in the workplace and feel that they must walk on eggshells. I had one male co-worker compliment a suit I had just purchased. Then he hurriedly apologized for the compliment, thinking I might view it as "sexist." When we are afraid to show, or to accept, kindness, we have truly gone too far.

Finally, a more insidious reason for denying women chances to develop has do to with power. Some men deny women (and other subordinates) chances to advance because they feel the need to retain a "one-up" power position over them. A particularly troublesome manifestation of this power struggle is sexual harassment. It has been long recognized that sexual harassment is not about sex. As Michael Crichton so eloquently wrote in his novel *Disclosure*, sexual harassment is about power. Even when men are already in the one-up position, some can't resist abusing that power by harassing the women who work for them.

A recent example is the dismissal of the CEO of W. R. Grace by the board of directors because of accusations of his repeated and wide-spread sexual harassment of female employees. While the board seemed to take the accusations seriously enough to dismiss him, they negated the impact of their action by giving him a salary and benefits severance package of more than $43 million — far more than re-quired by his contract. Even more outrageous is the fact that his be-havior had apparently been tolerated for quite some time, until he fell out of favor of the chairman for unrelated reasons. A *Wall Street Journal* article summed it up well, "The messy Grace affair shows how sexual harassment has been tacitly tolerated in some companies — and how it can be trotted out selectively as a cudgel."

Thus, for the many reasons outlined, women have not always been given the chances they need to gain business experience and develop leadership skills. Perhaps the "chance" that has the largest long-term impact on their careers is that women are rarely given the chance to fail. They are rarely put in the "stretch" jobs to which men are routinely assigned that allow them to be heroes — or to fail. Women are rarely fast-tracked and moved ahead before they are too comfortable in their jobs, the way men are.

I remember being promoted to director in a major aerospace corporation. From my perspective, the promotion was long overdue. I had been performing in that exact job for over six months, but my boss had not been forthcoming with the title or the salary. Imagine my surprise when upon the announcement of my promotion, one of my new peers said to me, "Your boss took a big risk putting you in this job." I saw no risk at all. He had been allowed to "try before you buy" for six months!

Women need to be allowed to take the same risks as men. They need to know that they can make the mistakes and still recover the same way men do. There's an old story about a manager at AT&T who was allowed to start up a new operation. He failed miserably and ended up losing over $7 million for the corporation. Summoned to the chairman's office, he was sure he was going to be fired for this terrible failure. Deciding that it was better to meet this head-on, the young man said, "Sir, I know you're going to fire me and I understand." "Fire you!", the chairman exclaimed, "I just spent $7 million training you!" The time is right for women to get this same training opportunity.

CHOICES WOMEN MAKE . . . AND DON'T MAKE

As much as it is incumbent upon corporations to give women the same chances as men, it is incumbent upon the women to invest in their own success. The current opportunities will result in success for those who make the sometimes difficult career choices that provide experience and visibility. The risk-takers and the fast-trackers of any gender work hard and work smart. They do what it takes to get the job done. They are positive about their ability and strike the words "no" and "can't" from their vocabularies. They travel, they relocate — whatever it takes. As men have always done, women who wish to get ahead must make these types of decisions and personal commitments — sometimes at a cost in other areas of their lives.

14

Women, more than men, are faced with choices between family and work. The choices women make determine, in large part, how fast and how far up the ladder they go.

There are two interesting and conflicting phenomena taking place right now. First, with the corporate downsizing and massive layoffs, most companies are asking employees to do more with less. There are simply fewer people to do the same amount of work, so companies are expecting their workers to work harder and longer.

At the same time, there is a shift in values and work ethic in two major segments of the work force. The young workers entering the work force, the so-called "Generation X" workers, do not have the same high expectations as their baby boomer counterparts. Expecting little and being critical of the apparent "work obsessiveness" of the older generation, they often do not choose to make the commitment and sacrifices expected of executive aspirants of the previous generation. The baby boomer professionals who have made the sacrifices to get ahead are facing the reality that many will not make it to the top. Many are recognizing that they are running out of time to have children, or that with the rush to get ahead they have not spent much time with the children they do have.

The need to balance careers with personal lives has become a major requirement for many in both groups. Thus, while corporations are demanding more and more, we now have a significant set of workers, both men and women, who are making choices to get off the fast track and add more balance to their lives.

I had lunch recently with a man who had been a general manager in a large corporation when I worked for him. Now he is a sales representative. What happened? He had children, and in his mid-forties, decided that he wanted to play an active role in their growing up. He made the choice to take a job in which he could work close to 40

15

*hours per week, probably about half the hours he and I
used to work when we worked together.*

**Even highly successful women find that at the end of a long and
busy day, they still are expected to handle most of the traditionally "female" duties around the home, whether this means to do
them themselves or hire them out.**

This dilemma, finding balance between work and family, has traditionally been a women's career challenge. Research has shown
that the impact of staying out of the workplace for a period of time
can be severe. A recent Department of Labor report compared female MBAs who left the work force to have children to those who
had no break in their service. When the women who had children
returned to work, they discovered that they were now making on
average 17% less than their counterparts who were childless or who
had their children and returned to work immediately. Additionally,
only 44% of the women with the break in service reached senior
middle management positions, while 60% of their counterparts who
continued to work did.

A survey of Fortune 1,000 female corporate officers, conducted
by Heidrick and Struggles, found that four of five survey participants
felt that they had made personal sacrifices because of career demands.
These sacrifices included time for themselves, their spouses, and their
children — if they had children. Over 50% of the women were childless, and one-third of them cited their careers as the reason why. Other
studies show that for women who stay in the game, the sacrifices are
continuous. The struggle to allocate time across multiple priorities
never goes away. Even highly successful women find that at the end
of a long and busy day, they still are expected to handle most of the
traditionally "female" duties around the home, whether this means to
do them themselves or hire them out. Even women who had what

they considered "exceptionally supportive" husbands claimed they got little help around the house.

Does this mean that we really can't have it all — a successful career, a family and leisure? Perhaps not. One recent study refutes some of the research cited above. Peter Capelli at the University of Pennsylvania, along with Jill Constantine of Williams College and Clint Chadwick of Wharton, found that high school graduates in 1972 who believed that it was very important to "find the right person to marry" and "have a good family life," 14 years later earned from 4 to 7% more than those who put less value on marriage and family. In fact, the study found that having a bad family life or poor marriage could be hazardous to one's career. "If you have a bad family life, that takes a lot of time. And it is an enormous distraction while trying to work on your career," according to Capelli.

Moreover, the shift in values has made many companies begin to rethink what they expect of their successful executives. Even with the demands within downsized organizations, many have found that it is in their best interest to allow their employees more flexibility in balancing their lives. Perhaps, over time, more companies will follow this path. When they do, the choices will become less difficult and the sacrifices less severe. However, the reality of the situation is that *today,* climbing to the top of the corporate world still involves intense competition and sacrifice. Therefore, the choices women make will continue to impact how fast, and often how far, they will go up the ladder.

That is not to say that women are faced with an absolute choice or a one-time decision. A female executive at a major aerospace firm made this point during a company sponsored "Women's Week." She encouraged women to make the choice that was right for them at that particular time and place in their lives. In other words, if you decide to slow roll things on the career front for a while, you can get back on the fast track later, when it's more right for you. In her case, she selected assignments that involved little travel while her children were small. Yet she is one of a very small number of vice presidents at this large firm. In another woman's case, she left the work force for over nine years to complete part of her education and be at home with her children. Despite this hiatus, she was able to re-enter the work force, complete a masters degree, run her own company, and make the senior management ranks of a major corporation.

Some women, especially those with solid support structures and supportive spouses, have been able to "have it all" without ever getting off the fast track. One woman who had a commuter marriage for a while tells about her choices:

> *Balancing, to me, is a matter of setting priorities and knowing when you must put family before work and work before family. Even though my office is in Virginia, when people ask me where I live, I tell them, "My family is in North Carolina." Sometimes they think I forget where I live. I am on the road a minimum of 50% of the time. To my family, it seems like more. But, when I'm in North Carolina, I spend time with my children, participating in their lives — Boy Scouts, Girl Scouts, dance, sports, and school events. I arrange teacher conferences and orthodontist appointments so that I can attend. On weekends, I don't worry about dirty rooms and unmade beds. I watch soccer games, go to the library, and spend time just being with my family. I have to stop and think about what is really important to me and my family in the scope of things. A clean house and home-cooked meals are not at the top of the priority list. I don't feel like I ever make sacrifices. I make choices.*

Her own success, like that of many other women, is evidence that our accomplishments result from the choices we make and the opportunities we exploit during our careers:

> *The woman in the aerospace company, once her children were older, was able to experience a major leap in her career when she and six men were considered for a key*

executive management position. She did her homework, found out who on the selection committee was undecided, and unabashedly lobbied her way into a position for which she was considered to be the least likely candidate by everyone involved.

My friend who decided to take a break to raise her children decided to gain equality through starting her own business. The experience she gained and the credibility she attained are key factors in the salary she commands and the positions she's offered at the large company where she now works.

I climbed the ladder by always volunteering for the hard, risky jobs no one else wanted, getting undeniable results, and by being willing to relocate at the drop of a hat. The impact on my personal life was substantial — I postponed marriage until I was nearly 40 years old and I chose to be childless — but I was one of the youngest vice presidents ever appointed in both of the companies I served.

The point is that the choices women make are important. They define where they will go and how they get there. During this exciting time, women have more opportunity than they've had in this century. What this opportunity means to each woman personally will be determined by the individual choices she makes. Women — as well as men — need to set goals, re-examine those goals frequently, and operate out of choice. Only then will they be able to look back with satisfaction and without regret.

Chapter Two

Playing to Your Strengths

The problem that has no name — which is simply the fact that American women are kept from growing to their full human capacities — is taking a far greater toll on the physical and mental health of our country than any known disease....

-Betty Friedan

BEING YOURSELF

Women have many strengths, but being a man is not one of them.

There was a time in the late 1970s and early 80s when a large number of women came to work dressed in pinstripe suits, starched shirts, and floppy bow ties. This ensemble was, of course, accompanied by "sensible" shoes, and, if any jewelry at all, a string of pearls and perhaps stud earrings. If you looked in my closet at the time, you would have found nothing but gray and navy blue suits, accompanying white blouses, and enough floppy bow ties to require their own little rack. I, like most of my female counterparts, was dressing like a "little man."

This was encouraged by John Molloy's *The Woman's Dress for Success Book*, in which he cautioned women not to carry handbags, take off their jackets at work, wear designer eyewear, or have anything feminine in their offices — all in an attempt to blend in with their dressing-for-success male counterparts. Confused and uncertain, with no feminine role models, many of these same women not only attempted to look like the men they worked with, they tried to act like them, in their language and their management styles.

The end result was that everyone, men and women alike, were uncomfortable. Women were suppressing their feminine sides and trying to be something they were not — *men*. The men were confused and uncertain of how to deal with this somewhat unpredictable being who didn't look or act anything like their paradigm of a woman. We were all miserable, and it took us many years to recover from this trying period. What we learned from this is:

- When we are uncomfortable with ourselves, we make others uncomfortable with us as well.
- We do our best work when we are satisfied with ourselves and happy with our environments.
- We should all play to our strengths, and being a man is not a strength for a woman.

COGNITIVE BRAIN DIFFERENCES AND GENDER-SPECIFIC STRENGTHS

Women's interactive brains allow them to think nonlinearly and to consider many possibilities when problem solving.

There was a period in time when it was argued (mostly by early feminists), that the only differences between men and women were their reproductive organs. Therefore, it was thought men and women were interchangeable in the work environment. Studies now show that men and women vary widely in their emotional makeup, approach to problem solving, and actually have physical differences in the way their brains process information.

As a result, it has been suggested that there are some characteristics common to most women regardless of personality type. These characteristics, once considered the "soft" skills, have now come of age in the business environment. These can be the strengths that make the difference for women if developed and channeled properly.

Research has been conducted on gender-related brain differences for almost two decades. Researchers and scientists, such as Dr. Benjamin Shaywitz at Yale Medical School; Sandra Witelson, a behavioral neuroscientist at McMaster University; and Ann Moir, a British Ph.D. in genetics, all drew similar conclusions about the differences between men's and women's brains. But only recently has the technology advanced to the point that these earlier hypotheses can be substantiated by hard science.

The invention of new magnetic resonance imaging (MRI) technologies, as well as observations made in autopsies, during brain surgeries, and after strokes, have supported the earlier theories that men's brains are more specialized and compartmented than women's and that women's brains are more generalized than men's.

Women have more connective tissue between the two brain hemispheres, allowing more interaction between the two sides during the thought process.

Studies show that when faced with the same problem to solve, men will use one localized portion of one side of their brains, while women will use a much more diffused range of tissues on both sides of the brain. It is believed that this is primarily due to the structural differences in men's and women's brains. Women, in general, have more connective tissue, or *corpus callosum*, between the two brain hemispheres, allowing more interaction between the two sides during the thought process.

This extra connective tissue is what allows young girls to develop language skills before their male counterparts, while the "compartmentalization" in the male brain allows young boys to develop spatial skills before their female counterparts. Boys eventually develop language skills, and girls eventually develop spatial skills; but the extent to which they do, and the manner in which they use these portions of their brains, continues to differ into adulthood.

Women's superior proximal senses allow them to process more sound, light, and pain data from their environments. This may account for the perception that women are more intuitive.

Other data show that females have the innate ability to receive a wider range of sensory information than their male counterparts and to connect and relate that information with greater ease. This superiority of women's proximal senses includes receiving and processing sound, light, and pain data. This may account for the perception that women are more intuitive. Instead, women merely are processing more data in their environments. It has also been found that, generally, women learn better through verbal communications, men through visual.

While the research continues and the results are hotly debated, this difference in functional brain organization is believed to be responsible for women's ability to consider multiple paths and multiple solutions. As women solve problems, their brains will process a variety of sensory, memory, and other data before they draw any conclusions; and then they may draw multiple conclusions. Their male counterparts will solve problems more linearly, using only one side of their brains, and will draw a single conclusion.

In her book *Office Biology*, Edith Weiner addresses this phenomenon, and notes that women "have a more interactive brain model" and "...women's brains may be likened to pinball machines, with thought traveling around, and lots of lights and possibilities going off, making and remaking connections." She speculates that women's diffused way of gathering and processing information may be why men tend to believe that women lack focus in problem solving.

Further research on men's and women's brain functions shows that, in general, women are more adept at remembering details, outscore men on tests requiring verbal skills, are better nurturers, and have superior fine-motor coordination. Men, on the other hand, generally outscore women on tests requiring mathematical reasoning, are better at representing three-dimensional structures mentally, and are better at some motor skills such as throwing and striking.

If we wish, as business people, to assemble truly effective teams in which the members fill gaps in each others' abilities and all aspects of a problem or situation are considered, we need teams of both men and women, preferably with styles covering the entire spectrum.

HUNTERS AND GATHERERS

The unique way women gather and process information can be used to their advantage in business.

To capsulize our differences, hundreds of years of socialization have not overcome millions of years of gene imprinting. Men are still better hunters, and women are still better gatherers. But there are few job openings today for hunters or gatherers, so how do women translate their innate skills to the current workplace? Personality differences notwithstanding, the general differences would indicate that women in business have the potential to be better verbal and written communicators, more adept at managing multiple facets in a changing business, more in tune with customers, and better managers of people — *exactly the skills needed to be highly successful in the information age.*

Communication skills. So much of success in business depends upon one's ability to communicate and sell ideas, both verbally and in writing. Employees who can present their ideas most effectively often get the best projects, the most funding, and the most visibility. They have more opportunity to impress others with their competence and their skills and to gain key assignments that will help them get ahead. Quite often, the only exposure many employees have to top management is in briefings, where communication skills are really put to the test. Having a natural tendency toward strong verbal and written communication skills is a key advantage.

Nonlinear thinking. Because, historically, there were no scientific data to back up why women typically came up with multiple solutions and multiple paths when problem solving, many creative thinkers were labeled "scatter-brained." We now know that a better term would be "whole brained," as women tend to draw on all of their brain resources to solve problems, rather than a small compartmented area. This ability to "think outside the box," if properly developed, can be a real asset in jobs requiring the ability to consider different points of view (e.g., managing, selling) and requiring creativity (e.g., strategic planning, product planning).

In today's complex business environment, the flexibility to approach a problem from numerous directions, to see the client's and competitor's points of view, to sense clients' reactions to proposals, can translate into getting to market better, faster, and more cheaply. In our highly competitive business environment, this could mean the difference between companies that succeed and those that don't.

People skills. The same skills that have allowed women to be good parents also allow them to be good coaches, salespeople, and managers. One reason many women have been extraordinarily successful in sales is that their innate ability to read people and respond to their needs has won them many clients. Client care surveys have shown over and over that many clients believe women listen to their requirements better than men and are more conscientious about responding to them. These clients had an overall feeling that they were more than just an account number to these sales reps, and that their business truly mattered and was appreciated.

The same skills that have allowed women to be good parents also allow them to be good coaches, salespeople, and managers.

Likewise, many people say they enjoy working for women because, as managers, women tend to be more "human oriented" and concerned about the employee as a person, not just someone who performs a job function. Women are more inclined to recognize personal events in an employee's life such as births, deaths, and employee birthdays. Many employees feel more "connected" to their female managers because of the time they are willing to spend getting to know them personally. This "connectedness" often can be a very real factor in employee motivation and satisfaction. Furthermore, women are more inclined than men to give honest, constructive performance feedback — something all of us need.

Because of women's people skills, they often are more adept at facilitating and helping a group reach consensus. With today's diverse workplace and self-managed workgroups, this skill is critical and women should hone it to perfection. Not only is consensus building an asset in managing an organization, but many companies value the skill so much today, and have such a difficult time finding it in their own organizations, they will pay large sums of money for professional facilitators to help them solve difficult problems or reach consensus in important meetings.

Information and power. Many men believe that information is power, and that by keeping the information to themselves, they increase their power base. Most women have figured out that to leverage themselves through others is where the real power is, and that in order to gain that leverage, they must inform and empower others. Therefore, women tend to share information more readily than men — which helps ensure that women managers' visions and goals are communicated and carried out more effectively. By empowering others with information and the ability to make their own decisions, women can push authority down in the organization. This results in quicker response time and higher organizational productivity.

Their own view of success. Ann Moir writes, "Boys and men live in a world of things and space, girls and women in a world of people and relationships." This perspective impacts everything women do, as well as how they define success and set and achieve goals. For the male, who is programmed to understand hierarchies and dominance, success is quantitative — it can be defined by the size of the organization, dollars of budget, numbers of papers published. Women, on the other hand, view each quantitative event as they view everything else — as part of a larger *qualitative* picture.

In 1992, women responded to a survey of the National Association for Female Executives on why they wanted to start their own businesses. The results of the survey were published in an October

1992 press release by *New Woman* magazine and the National Association for Female Executives. Wealth and fame, cited most often in other surveys by men, ranked dead last for women.

Instead, over three-quarters of respondents cited the desire to feel passionate about their work, the wish for emotional independence, the belief that they have something of value to market, and the conviction that they are doing something of value for others as the main reasons for starting their own businesses. While most women do want money, and certainly expect to be fairly compensated, money is not a woman's sole motivator or primary measure of success. Women measure success by the quality of their relationships and how they fit into and impact the big picture.

JUST THE FACTS

In management assessments, women outscored men when rated by employees, bosses, and themselves.

What do these differences between men and women mean in the burgeoning information age? To satisfy numerous queries from his clients, Larry Pfaff, president of Lawrence Pfaff and Associates, a human resources consulting firm, conducted research on 1,059 men and women in 211 organizations to ascertain the differences in their skills as managers.

The research was conducted by surveying over 6,000 individuals who were either peers, subordinates, or bosses of the subjects in question. The surveys contained questions regarding how the subjects performed in 20 categories of management, from goal-setting and planning to teamwork, self-confidence, and decision-making. Likewise, the subjects themselves were surveyed in order to determine how they viewed themselves in these categories.

The results were dramatic. Subordinates rated the women higher than men in 20 of 20 categories, bosses rated them higher in 19 of 20 categories, and the women rated themselves higher in 15 of 20 categories (Table 1). Since most of us care more about how our bosses view us than anyone else, it is important to note that of the 19 categories where women were rated higher by their bosses, 15 were statistically significant (Table 2). Some of the biggest gaps (on a scale of 1 to 100) were in evaluating the performance of employees, where women scored a 63 versus men's 53; planning, where women averaged a 55 versus a 48 for their male counterparts; facilitating change, 58 for women versus a 46 for men; communication, where women scored a 59 and men averaged 50; and decisiveness, where women averaged a score of 50 against the men's 44. Empowering employees and trust were two other areas where women averaged large spreads (10 points) above their male counterparts. The ratings by employees are similarly favorable to women and are shown in Table 3.

These data could be interpreted in one of two ways. One could surmise that in the categories assessed, or even in general, women really *are* better managers than men. If this were true, it would truly be groundbreaking, as many organizational cultures still support the notion that putting women in positions of power or leadership is inherently "risky." What if, in fact, putting women in these roles is actually less risky than putting men in them?

On the other hand, one could speculate that because of the barriers our corporate cultures create for women who try to reach the top, only the very excellent squeak by and become managers or leaders. If you subscribe to *this* idea, then one would expect these "superwomen" to shine compared to the average male who was relatively unhindered in his path up the ladder and was able to reach the same level by being mediocre or average instead of excellent.

What if women really are better managers, and putting them in positions of leadership is less risky than putting men in these roles?

Table 1						
Pfaff Study Shows Women are Rated Higher by Employees, Bosses, Selves						
Management Leadership Practices Factors	**Employee Ratings**		**Boss Ratings**		**Self Ratings**	
	Higher Rated M=Men W=Women	Statistically Significant* Y=Yes N=No	Higher Rated M=Men W=Women	Statistically Significant* Y=Yes N=No	Higher Rated M=Men W=Women	Statistically Significant* Y=Yes N=No
Goal Setting	W	Y	W	Y	W	N
Planning	W	Y	W	Y	W	N
Technical Expertise	W	N	--	N	M	N
Performance Standards	W	Y	W	Y	W	Y
Coaching	W	Y	W	Y	W	Y
Evaluating Performance	W	Y	W	Y	W	Y
Facilitating Change	W	Y	W	Y	W	Y
Delegation	W	N	W	N	--	N
Recognition	W	Y	W	Y	W	Y
Approachable	W	Y	W	Y	W	Y
Directive	W	Y	W	N	--	N
Participative	W	Y	W	Y	W	N
Strategy	W	Y	W	N	M	N
Communication	W	Y	W	Y	W	N
Teamwork	W	Y	W	Y	W	Y
Empowering Employees	W	Y	W	Y	W	Y
Trust	W	N	W	Y	W	Y
Resourcefulness	W	Y	W	Y	W	Y
Self-Confidence	W	N	W	N	M	N
Decisiveness	W	Y	W	Y	W	N

*The significance level for Table 1 indicates the probability that the measured difference would occur at random in a population of this size. The commonly accepted standard is to consider differences as statistically significant when the probability is 5% or less.

Female N=383 managers
Male N=676 managers

	Table 2		
	Bosses Rated Women Higher in 19 of 20 Categories		
FACTOR	**FEMALE** Percentile Score	**MALE** Percentile Score	**DIFFERENCE** Points
Goal Setting	59	51	8
Planning	55	48	7
Technical Expertise	50	50	0
Performance Standards	58	53	5
Coaching	59	49	10
Evaluating Performance	63	53	10
Facilitating Change	58	46	12
Delegation	52	50	2
Recognition	58	50	8
Approachable	59	49	10
Directive	52	50	2
Participative	54	48	6
Strategy	54	49	5
Communication	59	50	9
Teamwork	60	51	9
Empowering Employees	59	49	10
Trust	58	48	10
Resourcefulness	58	50	8
Self-Confidence	53	50	3
Decisiveness	50	44	6

Table 3			
Employees Rated Women Higher in 20 of 20 Categories			
FACTOR	**FEMALE Percentile Score**	**MALE Percentile Score**	**DIFFERENCE Points**
Goal Setting	57	50	7
Planning	56	46	10
Technical Expertise	55	52	3
Performance Standards	57	50	7
Coaching	56	49	7
Evaluating Performance	63	53	10
Facilitating Change	59	49	10
Delegation	55	54	1
Recognition	54	46	8
Approachable	54	50	4
Directive	56	50	6
Participative	56	50	6
Strategy	55	50	5
Communication	57	49	8
Teamwork	55	49	6
Empowering Employees	59	51	8
Trust	53	49	4
Resourcefulness	57	49	8
Self-Confidence	56	54	2
Decisiveness	52	45	7

I believe the true answer involves some of each interpretation. Women's innate skills, combined with the way that they are socialized, are *more* appropriate for grooming managers of knowledge workers than men's innate skills and the way that men are socialized. Women start with improved verbal and people skills and then are socialized to be coaches, facilitators, and gain consensus. They learn to get along, at home, at work, at play. Men, on the other hand, start with better spatial and motor skills, but are socialized to be aggressive, competitive, and vie for that one-up spot. Imagine the shock to a young man who has been taught for years to single-mindedly pursue his personal goals and wipe out all obstacles in his way. Suddenly, he is dropped into a business environment where he is expected to get along, share information, and be part of a decision-making team, rather than just concentrate on his individual success.

While many women were ill-equipped to get along in command-and-control environments, most men are likewise ill-equipped to adapt to the new management demands created by our new organizations of knowledge workers. So women *will* test higher, because they are testing skills that come naturally to them and are at odds with the way most men have been socialized to behave.

One executive in a particularly male-dominated environment shared how he had come to the conclusion — by a different path — that women were better suited for the role of managing knowledge workers.

I was in charge of the development and integration of a large office automation system for five Air Force bases across the country. The deployment of the five sites was time-phased over a fairly long period of time, so a number of personnel changes would naturally occur during this period. The first two site managers were men, but by the time all five sites were deployed, I noticed, much to my surprise, that all five site managers were women. Because this was so unusual, I decided to analyze how it came to be. I determined that in my efforts to keep this client happy,

I had put the people in the site manager jobs who could best handle the client. It turned out that the women were more "people oriented" versus the men who were more "cable oriented." That's what the client needed, so I had gradually migrated toward that solution without being conscious of the personnel mix.

The data — both scientific and anecdotal — suggest that a window of opportunity exists in today's workplace for women's skills to be appreciated and viewed as assets, not liabilities. Women should take advantage of this opportunity, while taking responsibility for ensuring that they are adequately educated, trained, and prepared to hold the key jobs they seek. The rest of this book is dedicated to helping women make the right choices and take the right steps to lead them to the opportunities they desire.

Chapter Three

Goal Setting and Career Planning

A safe assignment will not bring you to the notice of senior management. Look for places where you can make an impact. Seek out the challenges.

-Paul Stern

SETTING AND ASSESSING GOALS

Few people, be they men or women, stand a chance at top jobs without careful goal setting and focused career planning.

For years, there has been a lot of talk about the "glass ceiling" and many women's inability to break through it. Whether it was because of the time I entered the work force (about 20 years ago), or the industry I entered (engineering, aerospace), I have seen a tremendous amount of discrimination and resistance against women at every level and in almost every nonadministrative job. Surprisingly enough, the resistance has not only been from men. Many women tell stories of how their female staffs — secretaries, nurses, and other

37

support personnel — undermined them or blatantly gave preferential treatment to their male peers at their expense. Sad, but true. This internal resistance has been compounded by peers who stabbed women in the back, bosses who withheld information from them, and corporate cultures that were not "female friendly." There's a line in a popular song that rings true: "You can't go the distance with too much resistance." With all the resistance women have faced over the years, it's a small wonder that any women have risen to senior positions.

These practices and attitudes aren't entirely gone, but they certainly have gotten better over time, and I believe that the glass ceiling is quite a bit higher than it was 20 years ago. It still exists, however, and women must be smart about how to break through. Goal setting and focused and careful career planning can increase any woman's chances of making "the break." Without it few women, and few men, for that matter, stand a real chance at top jobs.

If you interviewed most senior executives, you would find that they have known for some time that they were destined for top jobs. They made careful and deliberate moves during their entire careers to position themselves for the jobs they now hold. Few, if any, believe that they "lucked into" the jobs. On the contrary, they worked extraordinarily hard, stayed very focused, and made numerous personal sacrifices to reach their goals. In fact, many of these executives were identified early in their career as "high potential" candidates, by companies who target this type of employee and provide formal programs to assist them in reaching their goals.

AT&T, for example, has a Management Development Program (MDP), wherein select, high-potential employees are assigned to high risk/high reward positions. As they succeed in those positions, they are moved to other positions exposing them to all facets of the business — marketing, operations, and engineering. The goal of the MDP is to establish a pool of well-rounded general management executives that the corporation can draw upon for its senior level succession program. The majority of AT&T executives today — men and women alike — came from the MDP program.

One woman talks about the use of her company's goal setting mechanisms:

> *I believe in self-fulfilling prophecies. If you go through life accepting what comes your way, that is exactly what will happen. We have to take control and make things happen. Think about and decide what you want to be when you grow up and set short- and long-term milestones. My company's performance evaluation form has sections for short- and long-range goals. It is surprising how many people have a hard time taking it seriously. I feel it's very important. I personally always have long- and short-term goals I am working toward. By long-term, I mean five to ten years. Short-term can mean anywhere from next week to next year. I am very fortunate — I have been able to meet and, in most cases, exceed my long-term goals that, all together, were my road to the position I hold now.*

The Glass Ceiling Commission, in its research on American corporations, compiled a list of factors common to successful executives:

- Broad and varied experience in the core areas of the business
- Access to information, particularly through networks and mentoring
- Company seniority
- Initial job assignment
- High job mobility
- Education
- Organizational savvy
- Long hours and hard work
- Career planning

It's hard to set goals when the organization keeps changing.

When most of the executives included in the study above selected their goals and began their plans to reach them, they worked in large, hierarchical organizations that were growing and expanding. Climbing the corporate ladder was a clearly definable path and success could be measured by the size of the organizations they managed and the budgets they controlled. With today's shifting economy, and with the reengineering of so many companies, it's much harder to find a clear path to the top and, in fact, even to define success. Organizations have gotten flatter and less hierarchical. Managers manage processes and workgroups, but often don't really control all of their own resources anymore. Even more frustrating, with the reengineering and flattening of organizations, it is possible to aspire to and work toward a position that may not even exist when you get there.

These changes must be considered when setting goals today. It's not adequate merely to copy what worked in the past. The key to goal setting and career planning in this highly dynamic and ever-changing environment is to maintain flexibility and be willing to revamp your definition of success as the organizational structure changes. What hasn't changed amid all the other turmoil is the need to define goals, determine paths, and take the appropriate risks to get there.

Goal setting is still easiest when starting from the end point and working backward. Goals should be well-defined and quantifiable. For example, *"I want to be CEO of a Fortune 500 company before I am 55 years old."* Intermediate milestones can then be established to help ensure the success of the longer-term goal. *"In order to do this, I will need to be an operations vice president before I am 40, and a division president by the time I am 45."*

Detailed career plans, regarding intermediate assignments, education, visibility needed, performance criteria that must be met, and other factors germane to the environment in which an executive works can then be built around these goals. Again, a word of caution. In many companies, the positions themselves may change over time as an executive works toward them, and the intermediate milestones may vary considerably. Candidates should be aware of the shifts in organizations and maintain flexibility in their thinking as they work toward their goals.

The key to goal setting and career planning in this highly dynamic and ever-changing environment is to maintain flexibility and be willing to revamp your definition of success as the organizational structure changes.

One woman had set a goal so far in the future that she had consciously forgotten about it until it was reached:

> *I was 21 years old when I met a man in my company who was 35 and a vice president. While he was clearly bright and personable, I remembered thinking that he wasn't really extraordinary, just focused. I can do that, I thought — be a vice president in a Fortune 500 company by the time I'm 35. I don't remember being conscious of this particular goal over the next 13 years, but clearly it was in my subconscious. I was appointed vice president in a $20 billion dollar company two months before my 35th birthday. As I signed my acceptance letter, I remembered back to 13 years earlier when I had set the goal.*

While I recommend being more "consciously competent" in goal setting, having subconscious goals is better than not having them at all!

When setting goals, the following should be considered:

- **Are my goals realistic?** No one can set your goals for you, but others can certainly help you test them for realism. When setting goals for myself, I found it helpful to seek out those who held or had held the kinds of positions I desired for myself. I asked what kinds of experience were needed and what background people in senior positions had. After getting to know the executives, I asked about the kinds of things they recommended I do to be considered for these jobs. I found that this testing of the waters was helpful in determining whether to pursue senior management roles or move on to an environment where I had a better chance. Additionally, I discovered the kinds of experiences I needed to succeed.

This kind of reality checking is only useful if you are willing to listen not only to the advice, but also be perceptive enough to pick up the cues regarding your likelihood of success. You may not have the background for the job or the means to get the experience or the training required in the time frame needed to put you on track for your goal, or it may not be realistic for other reasons. Seeking out people who have been in the position you aspire to or who now manage that position can provide key insights.

Likewise, observe the time frames others have required to get to the job you desire and assess the realism of your time frames. Additionally, ensure that the intermediate milestones you have established are indeed the ones needed to get to your ultimate goal. This can be done by studying how others have reached the goal you desire, by interviewing people who are already there, and by getting advice from others, such as your boss, or your human resources department. It is essential that your goals be realistic and achievable in order for you to remain motivated and focused.

- **Am I willing to do the things required to reach this goal?** Reaching certain goals requires periods of intense focus and, perhaps, sacrifice. It may require long hours that keep you away from your family and other interests. It may require further education, heavy travel, or perhaps even relocation. You must be clear on what is required and what you are willing to do. It may be possible that you can alter some of these parameters, shorter hours or less travel, for instance, if you are willing to wait longer to reach your goals. All goals come with a cost attached in terms of effort and sacrifice. Smart goal setters "count the costs" ahead of time and make informed decisions with respect to their willingness to incur these costs.

Women, especially, seem to suffer here when it comes to families. They tend either to forgo having families at all, or feel overcome with guilt during times when they place their families behind their careers in terms of priorities. John Gray, in his book *What Your Mother Couldn't Tell You and Your Father Didn't Know*, discusses some of the reasons women still are expected, by themselves, and to some extent by their husbands, to carry most of the load around the household, from nurturing to cleaning. Gray offers women some suggestions for how to get more help and support from their husbands, but he cautions them that "men can only give more in small degrees." This added load of managing the household and family after putting in 50-60 hours per week has made many women think twice about the costs of "having it all." Make informed decisions and then move forward.

One woman told me a story about when she first started to do heavy business travel. Thinking it was no big deal, she missed her son's first band concert. Later, she found out it was indeed a big deal. After that, she made sure her children communicated to her what was really important and what was not, so that she could make appropriate choices. Acknowledging that you just can't do it all, she learned how to make appropriate choices.

- **When I reach this goal, will it be what I really wanted?** It's exciting to dream and plan for a goal, but the goal setter must understand what actually is required to stay there, once the goal is achieved. If your goal is to be director of marketing, you should observe the person in that job now. Does he or she have the work hours and the lifestyle you desire? Are you willing to work the hours, do the travel, attend the meetings, and keep the pace? Many people dream of being CEO of a major corporation or perhaps running their own company. Surveys have shown that for the most part, these people eat, sleep, and breathe their jobs. Their jobs are their lives. A recent *Fortune* article profiled several Fortune 500 CEOs. On average, these people worked 69 hours per week, slept 6.4 hours per night, traveled 12 days per month, and took only 13.5 days of vacation per year.

More specific to women, the Heidrick and Struggles survey mentioned in Chapter One found that the typical female corporate officer had these attributes:

-- Is a 44-year-old white Protestant employed at the vice president-level or above
-- Has worked for three employers thus far in her career
-- Devotes 55 hours per week to work
-- Is married, childless, and devotes less than 10 hours per week to homemaking tasks
-- Believes the increase in the number of self-employed women is the result of management's continued discomfort with women in executive positions (see Chapters One and Fifteen)
-- Thinks many high-achieving women forgo having chidren to stay on the fast track
-- Would not choose to stay home, even if paid a full salary to do so

As you set goals, it's important that you make sure that you understand and can live with all aspects associated with achieving them.

- **Is this the right goal for this time and place in my life?**
  Many of us are willing to do certain things at one point in our lives that we may not be willing to do at other points. For instance, most people with small children don't wish to do a tremendous amount of travel; however, before the children are born or after they are old enough to stay alone, heavy travel may be acceptable. Lifestyle choices, current circumstances, and personal needs should be factored into your goals. Many people have found that they can take a break from constantly striving toward their goals for periods in their careers — indeed, even take breaks from the workplace entirely for periods of time due to illness or family matters — and pick back up where they left off. With the faster pace in our lives today, and with many of us having to take care not only of children, but often parents as well, companies have learned that it is more cost-effective to give employees leaves of absence and take them back later than to retrain a totally new employee.

There was a woman who worked for me who came to us through the acquisition of the company for which she worked. She was very skilled at what she did, and we went to great pains to ensure that her transition was smooth so that she wouldn't be part of the "breakage" of the acquisition. I thought all was going well until she entered my office one day to tell me that she was accepting employment elsewhere. She had just gotten married and was focused on starting a family. Currently, she worked 10-12 hour days and had a long commute. With her new focus in life, the situation was no longer acceptable to her. She opted for a part-time job near her home.

PLANNING YOUR CAREER

Planning your career is your responsibility. It is too important to entrust to anyone else.

Once you have your goals clearly defined, it is time to put together a career plan that supports them. First and foremost, understand that planning your career and implementing the plan is *your* responsibility. No matter how good your boss, your mentor, or your human resources department is, no one cares about your career as much as you do. You *must* take charge and make it happen.

Begin by honestly assessing your current skills or having them formally assessed, and sketch out what you believe to be a series of assignments that will give you the skills and depth and breadth needed to reach your goal. Observe others and their paths, discuss it with people you trust who have already made the journey, discuss it with your human resources department or your boss. Understand the difference between line and staff jobs and what mix of the two you need to be successful. Some companies offer career planning kits to help with this process. Use whatever tools you have available.

I was once given the choice of two different jobs. One was to be the executive assistant to the number-three person in a Fortune 20 company. The other was to manage a small, self-contained software company that reported at a lower level. I was really torn about which job to take. I had been at a director level for three years and felt that I was ready for the move to vice president. I knew that my choice of jobs would have a significant impact on my progress to the next level. The executive assistant job would give me high-level exposure, international experience, and a spot at the corporate headquarters. The general manager job would give me profit and loss experience (which I'd already had, but not in that company) and would increase

46

my technical and financial management skills. Uncertain of what to do, I called the most senior woman in the company, whom I had met at a women's forum, and asked for her advice. "Oh that's easy!" she said. "Always take the line job over the staff job." While I believe you have to balance the line with the staff jobs, in this instance, she was right. I made vice president within the year.

A recent article by Laura Walbert in *CFO* magazine discusses why so few women in Fortune 500 companies make it to CFO. Their primary reason, she claims, is that women in finance gravitate to treasury and other staff positions rather than grab the line positions they need in order to get the top jobs. Why do women do this? Women gravitate to where there is the least resistance. In finance, this is to treasury and other "back room" staff jobs. Says Walbert, "There are fewer barriers to entry for women on the treasury side. Treasury is the one area in finance that's almost genderless because of its emphasis on results." Unfortunately, the "least resistance" jobs don't allow women to accumulate the experience in networking and interfacing required for jobs at the top.

Jobs that contribute most to the company's bottom line will get you further faster — but only if you perform well in them.

Understand what the high-impact jobs are in your company — the jobs that are in the mainstream of the corporation, not a subsidiary or a fringe business, and the jobs that contribute most to the company's success. Choose assignments that will give you visibility, will broaden your skills, and in which you will be successful. How do you do this? Study the company's annual report. Read the CEO's message. Read the corporate mission statement or any other direction or strategy that comes out of the corporate office. These statements will usually tell you where the company is making money and what top management wishes to emphasize. That's where you want to be — right in the thick of things.

Next, determine which assignments are key and which ones you are qualified to perform. If you are lacking training or experience to handle these assignments, figure out how to get what you need to be successful in each of them. Do you need to read a book? Take a class? Attend a seminar? Make the investment. In our continuously changing environment, *continuous learning* is the only way anyone can survive, much less get ahead. Sometimes, you will need to take a lateral assignment to gain needed experience. Do not hesitate to step sideways if, in the end, it will help you get where you want to go.

Deborah Hopkins of Unisys was the only woman vice president of finance in her company. She dared give up her title to become a program manager of a new check imaging product. While it was difficult for her to deal with co-workers' speculation that she was "kicked out of her job," her line experience has given her opportunities in the company she would not have had otherwise.

If you're truly aiming for a senior executive or general management job, assignment selection will be key to your success. You will ultimately need experience in marketing, operations, and finance, as well as a mix of line and staff jobs. Ultimately, what makes or breaks an executive is the breadth and depth of assignments she has had and the learning that has occurred in each assignment. Early assignments usually develop technical skills and operational competencies, while later assignments usually develop management and leadership skills.

Consider this carefully when planning your path. Make sure that you get assignments that allow you to gain experience in all three functional areas to develop your operational competencies — and balance line and staff assignments to develop your management and leadership competencies. If you can't actually get assignments that allow you to gain experience in all three functional areas, gain it in two of the three and figure out how to get a working knowledge of the third. This might be obtained from training, task forces, or special short-term assignments. The ideal situation is to gain functional experience while balancing the line and staff experience. Target your desired training opportunities and aggressively pursue them. It's not likely that they will happen for you otherwise.

GAINING SUPPORT FOR YOUR PLAN

Your career plan will not be successful without the support of others.

Once you have your goal, a basic career plan, and a basic developmental plan in place, it is time to test them and gain support from others who will play an important role in your success. The primary "other" in this picture is your boss. He or she needs to know what you want to accomplish in order to help you get there. Your boss can provide valuable advice on the realism of your goals, their timetables, the career plan that supports them, and the development needed for each interim assignment. *You must gain the support of your boss in order to get the needed training and assignments to reach your goal.* If, for some reason, your relationship with your boss is not such that you can gain this support, you must work to get out from under this individual and get reassigned to someone who will provide you the developmental opportunities you need. Your human resources department can help you with this and should keep this information confidential and work with you to get you reassigned.

Even when your boss is very supportive, it is essential to build a relationship with your boss' boss. This person is your window to the future and, most likely, will be the one who makes the decision on the promotion that will make you your boss' peer. Even if your boss is a big advocate of yours, at times your boss will stand in the way of your progress because of your importance to the group's success. Make sure you have the higher level relationship established.

As you work through your career plan over the years, you must always keep your bosses and your human resources department informed of where you are in your career plan and what your goals and expectations are. Gain an understanding from your immediate boss of how long you are expected to remain in an assignment before moving on. Gain commitment to help you move when that period of time is up. Understand also what is expected from you before you will be allowed to move on. Do you have to complete a project? Groom your successor? Make sure you leave nothing to chance.

PERFORMANCE AGAINST YOUR PLAN

You must perform well in every assignment. If you do not, everything else is for naught.

You must constantly test the realism of the plan and your strengths and weaknesses. Solicit feedback from your boss and your peers as to how your performance is viewed by others. Then work hard to eliminate weaknesses and develop new strengths. *Above all, you must perform well in every assignment.* Nothing will derail you faster than poor performance. This is especially important for women, as Dr. Judy Rosener points out in her book, *America's Competitive Advantage: Utilizing Women as a Management Strategy.* Based on years of primary research in corporate America, Dr. Rosener has determined that men — particularly white men — are assumed to be competent until they prove their incompetence. Women, on the other hand, are assumed to be incompetent and continually must prove otherwise. Unfortunately, one visible disaster may be used against you over and over again.

What do I mean by good performance? It is more than simply getting the job done. It is getting it done better than the people who have done it before. It is completing your assignments in a timely manner with quality output, while building the networks and relationships that make you effective.

Truly efficient people have learned that a high percentage of things that cross their desks can be discarded, yet others must be responded to immediately — and they know the difference.

There are some components of competency in performance that must not be overlooked. It is imperative that you answer mail and return phone calls in a timely manner. This is your primary link to other organizations and to your customers and is very visible. You cannot afford to look sloppy or disorganized in this regard. Do not let letters go out with typos and do not leave phone calls unanswered more than a day, at most. I had one job where I averaged over 100 phone calls per day. I sorted them by time zone so that I could return them all before I left for the day.

Briefings are another area in which you must always look well-prepared and in control. Practice your presentations out loud before you give them. Make sure you have anticipated as many of the questions the audience may have as possible. Understand what the audience knows and doesn't know, and put things in context for them. Above all, be in command of your subject matter and make sure your handout materials are neat and professional. (See also Chapter Ten on communicating.)

So how do you do all this and the rest of your job without working 100 hours a week? We've all seen people whose offices are a shambles. They are always behind, appear overworked and frazzled, and never return phone calls or messages. Yet the person next door, in essentially the same job, is cool, calm, and up-to-date on everything. What's the difference? The person next door has learned to prioritize and to delegate. Truly efficient people have learned that a high percentage of things that cross their desks can be discarded, yet others must be responded to immediately. They know the difference between the two. They also know how to work quickly and efficiently and how to delegate when appropriate.

If you are the former person and not the latter, consider taking a time management course or asking your boss to help you prioritize your current load. You must ultimately project the aura of being able to handle your current assignment and level of responsibility well before you can realistically be considered for a higher level or more complex job.

If you find yourself in an assignment for which you are truly ill prepared, determine what is needed to help you perform better. Is it training? Take a class — even on your own time and with your own money. Is it lack of contacts? Learn to network and dedicate some time to building alliances that can help you. Is it a learning curve problem? You may have to work nights and weekends until you can catch up and keep up. No matter what effort it takes, it is worth it, if you are serious about making your goal. Poor performance in any assignment, especially a very visible one, will take years to erase from people's memories.

MENTORS

Having a mentor can make the difference between a career that's moving and one that's stalled.

All along the way, one of the most helpful things that a goal-oriented career person can have is a mentor. Sometimes your mentor is your boss, but often he or she is not. A mentor is someone who has already traveled the path you are attempting to travel and can give you much needed advice and counsel on its pitfalls. A mentor is someone who cares enough about you to tell you when your goals are unrealistic and to offer constructive criticism when you need it. A mentor will help you navigate through treacherous political waters and help you spot derailers before you slide off the track. A Heidrick and Struggles survey of corporate women officers found that over

80% of them had had one or more mentors or sponsors. It made a difference.

There are two kinds of mentoring: "invisible mentoring" and "visible mentoring." Invisible mentoring is primarily advice and counsel from people you trust. They are people with experience and business savvy beyond what you currently possess. They act as a sounding board for your ideas and help you identify weaknesses in your performance or your career strategy. Invisible mentors may or may not be in your company. They can be friends, relatives, business acquaintances, people you meet in trade associations, or anyone who has an opportunity to observe how you communicate and interact with others in a business environment. Their motivation for mentoring is usually friendship.

Visible mentors assume some risk for your performance in terms of credibility with their peers. Don't let them down.

Visible mentoring is more complicated, because it involves people in your company who openly sponsor you. They not only give you advice and counsel, they recommend you to others for high profile assignments and promotions. Their motivation varies. Some people do it because grooming the next generation of executives is the right thing for the company. Others do it for the sense of personal satisfaction of helping someone else — sometimes as payback for all the help they received. Other times they will agree to mentor you because they *didn't* receive all the help they needed and don't want others to have to go through their careers without help and guidance.

Whatever their reason, by being "visible mentors," they assume some risk for your performance in terms of credibility with their peers. If you perform poorly in an assignment for which they recommended you, their eye for talent is called into question. Be aware of this, and if you are fortunate enough to have a "visible mentor," don't let him or her down.

How do you find a mentor? Invisible mentors are easier, because you can, and should, have many and they can be found nearly anywhere. Husbands, brothers, sisters, or friends can partially fill this role, as can friends and contacts made through professional associations. What's most important here is that your mentor has an opportunity to observe you and give you sound feedback and advice.

Finding visible mentors is somewhat harder, because the expectation is that they will openly sponsor you in the corporation — which means they must be comfortable that when they do, you will perform in a manner that reflects well on them. The best way to develop this kind of relationship is to be visible to these individuals.

- Invite them to lunch to share an idea with them.
- Discuss an upcoming presentation and get their advice.
- Ask them to play devil's advocate on a strategy you are developing
- Give them an opportunity to see how you work and how you think.
- Leave them with the impression that you are skilled and competent and that openly sponsoring you is risk-free.

Many companies are waking up to the fact that valuable female executives are slipping through the cracks because of the lack of a mentor or sponsor — and are taking action. Pacific Bell, the regional Bell operating company on the West Coast, has implemented a formal mentoring program that pairs high-potential women with senior executives. Hopefully, other companies will follow suit to protect their investment in their female resources. The only downside to formal mentoring programs is that, because they are somewhat "forced," sometimes the all-important chemistry is not there. Even if you get the opportunity to participate in a formal mentoring program, it is a good idea to have your own mentors on the side.

Sometimes having a mentor of the opposite sex is more challenging for both parties than same-sex mentoring, but in a predominantly male business environment, women need male mentors. There just aren't enough women to go around.

Mentoring is one area where gender seems to make a tremendous difference. Many men strike up mentoring relationships on the golf course or racquetball court — but few women are invited to one-on-one activities away from the office. And when they are, often eyebrows are raised. It's difficult for men and women who want to mentor someone of the opposite sex to find a suitable activity away from the office where they can relax and get to know each other without creating discomfort for either party or stirring up gossip.

One male managing partner in a consulting company routinely takes his male staff members to dinner one-on-one, but he is not comfortable doing the same with his female staff members. Some men are not comfortable having dinner with a woman, even when the woman is the boss.

In one job I had, I often took the female managers who worked for me to dinner, but my male managers, who were all married, were not comfortable having dinner with a "woman" and declined every time I invited them. I never knew that it was an issue until one male manager brought it up and expressed a desire to find an alternative way for him to get some private time "with the boss." We talked through it and finally decided that a long lunch would be a good substitute. Another man decided he would be comfortable having drinks after work, as long as he made it home for his regular dinner time. By communicating with each other and working through the issue, we found a solution that was comfortable for everyone.

Because it's often difficult to find common ground for men and women to socialize, network, and mentor each other, many women have flocked to golf as a nonthreatening arena for this kind of mingling. Once a nearly all-male bastion, the links are increasingly becoming a coed territory. By taking up golf, women are able to participate in client and company outings where they were previously excluded. Many women are surprised to learn that these outings are big social events used to build relationships, and that the skill of the golfer is of no real concern at most of them. One woman who had recently taken up golf commented, "If I'd known how bad most golfers are, I'd have taken up the game much sooner!"

Women should continue to do things that will put them in a position to be mentored by men, but even when they are, sometimes that special bond that only same-gender mentoring offers is missing. One female partner in a consulting firm tells this story:

> *I was out of town working at a client site. I had some things I needed to pick up at the mall before I met the team for dinner. One of the senior managers also expressed an interest in going to the mall before dinner, so she and I went ahead of the team, did our shopping, and met up with the other people at the restaurant. Going to the mall gave me a chance to spend some time alone with this woman and get to know her better, and in a different way than being at the client offices with her. Later at dinner, the woman remarked, "You don't know how much this means to me." Not being sure what she meant, I asked her to explain. She went on to say that in her particular consulting office, there were no female partners, so to get the opportunity to really spend some one-on-one time with a partner, followed by dinner, was really special for her. I hadn't realized until that moment how difficult it is for many women to find someone who is comfortable mentoring them. Most men aren't, and most women aren't in a position to do so.*

When women are in a position to mentor other women, it is essential that they do so. Women are in a unique position to help each other overcome some gender specific obstacles with which men, try as they might, are not able to assist. Women also can share that comfort level of women-helping-women similar to what men have shared with each other for so many years.

TO STAY OR NOT TO STAY

Sometimes it's necessary to change companies in order to stay on the fast track; but if you must, do so carefully and be aware of the downside.

Over time, some people feel a sense of frustration or anger with their jobs or companies that becomes intolerable, and they perceive they have no choice but to quit and move to another company. Sometimes the problem is that with massive layoffs, the survivors are working too long and too hard without a break. Other times, employees feel that they have worked hard, made significant sacrifices, and received little or no recognition for their efforts. Still others feel that they have poor relationships with their peers or bosses that are irreparable. Women often feel that they have found themselves in a company that is not "female friendly" and can't go as far as their potential would otherwise take them.

Many times people who suffer from these problems at work feel that by starting over in a new company they can get a break, some breathing room, and a fresh start. That may be true, but changing companies also has a significant downside, including loss of benefits based on tenure, loss of that very important internal network, having to rebuild credibility, and having to learn a new culture and new set of politics. For women, especially, because they are considered "incompetent" until proven competent, changing companies means proving themselves all over again, regardless of the level at which they start. Remember, also, it is difficult for women to build networks in most companies and to find mentors. Take all of these things into consideration when evaluating a change.

> *I had changed companies before, but at a much lower level. I had observed men entering our company at the level I was at now and saw that they had instant credibility. I remembered this as I considered making a move. I did finally decide to make the move and was surprised when, in my new company, I had to prove myself over again. I had over 15 years experience at that time, but when my credibility was questioned and I referred to my background, I was told that while I may have done all those things, I didn't "do them here." What bothered me the most about that was that I never heard anyone say that about or to any of the men, many of whose credentials were nowhere near mine.*

If you are considering leaving, examine whether you are really desperate to leave the company, or are needing a change in scenery or a jump start for your career. Will a short leave of absence allow you to refocus and re-energize? Most companies have a policy for leave of absence of up to 30 working days that, when combined with weekends, can total almost six weeks. I know two different women who thought they wanted to leave their companies because of varying levels of frustration and burnout. Both of them, after a reasonable period away, had time to reflect on their jobs and their companies, and both returned refreshed with renewed commitment to their careers.

Not all women who get frustrated or burned out can afford leave without pay. If you find yourself at the end of your rope, but without the financial wherewithal to take a serious break, try to work out something with your boss where you can take a short-term break by way of a task force or other temporary assignment that gives you a change of scenery. If the company and your boss realize that the alternative is to risk losing you, they will usually try very hard to accommodate your needs. Good business people know that burning out their employees is not productive and replacing them is not cost-effective. You must take responsibility, however, for communicating to your management chain that you are approaching burnout. Many bosses don't experience this personally and don't know the signs in others.

Often, companies stereotype or undervalue long-term employees based on assignments they have been in too long or mistakes they have made in the past. This can be a significant career roadblock. If you are not a "player," consider moving on.

There is another reason to evaluate staying with your company versus leaving for a new one. If you are interested in getting ahead in your company, you should periodically test the waters there to make sure you are viewed as someone who has the potential to get where you want to go. Are you viewed as a "player?" Someone on the fast track? If not, and it is not a situation you can career plan or mentor your way out of, you should consider changing companies. It's not uncommon for someone to be undervalued at a firm where they have been for a number of years. Often, people are stereotyped based on assignments they have gotten stuck in over time or from a former career setback or visible mistake that has not been forgotten. These types of situations can make it nearly impossible to shake an old or unfavorable image and can hold you back, as illustrated by this story:

> *There was a man I worked with once who supported my organization. He was highly educated and was excellent at his job. Based on his performance and skill base, he would easily have performed well in his second level boss' job. For some reason, the company seemed to have forgotten about him. I worked hard to get his boss to promote him to the next level, and he finally did, but for him*

to make up the two or three levels I felt he was behind, he would have had to leave the company. Because of where he was in his personal life — he had two small children and wasn't interested in heavy travel or relocating — he decided to stick it out.

Some industries — and specific companies inside those industries — are more "female friendly" than others and will offer more opportunities for women.

Some women feel that they are in companies that are not "female friendly." The culture may be so male-dominated that women, regardless of credentials or past performance, are forced to prove themselves over and over again to the point of exhaustion. These women often wish to make a move to companies that are more diverse and flexible and will offer them equal opportunities. If you are in this situation, consider a service company — banking, real estate, or insurance, for instance — or a retail company. Such firms have proven over time to be more "female friendly," constructing fewer barriers for women than other industries. Industrial companies that are more market-driven, produce consumer products, and have large customer bases of women and minorities, tend to provide better working environments for women than other industrials, but are still not as favorable as most service companies.

If finding a more "female friendly" environment is your reason for wanting to make a move, carefully research the company and industry you are considering — don't repeat the same mistake. Ask about the total number of women, women managers, and female officers. Make sure the culture values diversity, as opposed to feeling pressured into it.

For whatever reason you choose to do so, changing companies has good points and bad points that should be considered. The good points include more money and usually a promotion, as well as a chance to start over in a new environment with new challenges. Often, the same stressors that were sending you over the edge in the old company don't look nearly as bleak when associated with new names and faces. Changing companies also allows you to leave behind old baggage from past failures or missteps.

I am dismayed by all the stories from recruiters who say that women turn down plum assignments because they are risk-averse, while men grab the assignments and never look back.

The downside issues of benefits loss and break in service mentioned above can usually be compensated for in terms of salary and perks, but the less tangible downside of having to rebuild your alliances and networks and having to reprove your competency is significant and will require large amounts of focus and energy. I don't want to discourage women from taking these risks — on the contrary, I am dismayed by all the stories from executive recruiters who say that many women turn down plum assignments for these very reasons, while men grab the jobs and never look back. However, I do want women to know what they are up against and manage the risks. Weigh the pluses and minuses and decide what is best overall.

Sometimes different divisions of the same company act like different companies, and an internal move can result in most of the benefits but fewer of the negative aspects.

When considering leaving your company, see if you can accomplish the same thing by moving to a different part of your current company. Sometimes different divisions of the same company act like different companies, and an internal move can result in most of the benefits but fewer of the negative aspects. If it's still not possible to get what you want, prepare your resume and start looking, but accept nothing that doesn't get you back on the fast track.

I try not to say never, but *never, ever* take a cut in pay or a lesser job unless you are consciously trying to take a less demanding job or get off the fast track for a while. I have seen managers try to convince people, especially women, to take a job smaller in scope or with smaller salary to "get in the door." The women get there and find that others who are less technically skilled, but apparently better negotiators, got raises and promotions to come aboard. The employee is then resentful and angry and always behind her peers.

I don't know why hiring managers ever do this — it is not win-win — but I've seen it too many times. If faced with this situation, ask what the salary range and midpoint for the position are. If you are over the midpoint, you are probably overqualified for the position and ought to be negotiating for the next higher one. If you are below the midpoint, there is certainly no reason why you can't get an increase for changing companies, especially if you have lost benefits such as vacation or sick leave. Often, it is even possible to negotiate a signing bonus to make up for a benefits differential.

Titles, during a change, also should be looked at carefully. Understand which titles accompany which positions in each company. A director in a $4 billion company may have much more responsibility and command a much higher salary than a vice president in a $4 million company. Understand a title change in the context of the culture you are leaving and the culture to which you are moving.

When changing companies, negotiate carefully for your starting salary. I feel like I'm caught in a time warp when I hear stories of how much less women are offered for the same jobs as men, even when they have identical credentials. There were many articles published recently about a female surgeon at Columbia Medical School who found, much to her surprise, that her starting salary of $60,000 was substantially less than those of her male peers who graduated with her. Same degree, same schools, but the men began their careers at $100,000. It took her five years and a lot of pushing to get her salary up to $100,000, and, of course, the men's salaries did not stand still during that period.

Salary discrepancies like that are hard to recoup. Ask to see the salary range for the job. If you are fairly new in the field or at that level, you should be somewhere below the midpoint, but well within the range. If you have been at the position for some time, you should be above the midpoint. Do your homework before negotiating the offer and understand the company's strategy for giving incentives to its employees. Understand the mix of salary versus bonus versus benefits and carve out a package that is fair and equitable.

Do not settle for less than you are worth. Women have sold themselves short for too long.

Chapter Four

Managing, Leading, and the Bosses Who Do

The problem with many organizations,
and especially the ones that are failing,
is that they tend to be over managed and under led.

-Warren Bennis

Great necessities call forth great leaders.

-Abigail Adams

MANAGING VERSUS LEADING

In today's world of knowledge workers, executives need to be both effective managers and strong leaders.

I had a manager who worked for me once who really tried my soul. He was insubordinate, believed rules were for everyone other than himself, put the company at significant risk, and spent the company's money like a "drunken sailor." After several counseling sessions over many months, where I told him in no uncertain terms what was expected of him, and he told me in no uncertain terms that he didn't really care what I thought or wanted of him, I put him on probation with the intention of firing him as soon as possible. One day I was talking to one of his subordinates for whom I had a lot of respect. This young man praised his boss to no end. I was truly shocked, as I was of the opinion by that point that my problem employee had no redeeming characteristics. I decided to explore this further with the young employee by asking him to describe some of the things that he liked about his boss. What I was finally able to ascertain was that this man was a good leader, which is what his subordinates saw, but that he was a poor manager, which is what I saw. This situation brought home vividly to me that to be successful in today's corporations, you must be able both to lead and to manage.

Lead your people. Manage your business.

Leadership and management *are* different, and they are both important to a successful career. Managers focus more on the quantitative aspects of the business, while leaders focus more on the qualitative. In order to run an effective organization that produces both short- and long-term results, you have to be concerned about both numbers and people. Historically, the terms manager and leader have been used interchangeably, but I believe they require different skills and produce different results. As an example, one cannot "manage" a group of soldiers up a hill in the face of near-certain death. Conversely, one cannot "lead" the organization's assets to a better bottom line.

Because working for a corporation is a voluntary proposition, and most highly educated and highly skilled knowledge workers can easily find other jobs, successful leaders of these people must win commitment from them in order to keep them in their organizations. Today's leader needs to do this by:

- Communicating
- Seeking others' ideas — encouraging participation
- Getting buy-in on decisions impacting the group
- Building trust
- Inspiring
- Selecting great people for key jobs
- Empowering
- Following through on commitments

Leaders must not only possess these attributes, they must also be visionaries with a clear idea of where they want to go. They must communicate this vision to others and excite them about it enough to make them want to be a part of it. They must understand the importance of gaining the support of their troops and have a sense of presence or charisma that makes others want to follow. Today's leaders know that they can accomplish their mission only through others, and they value the effort and support they receive from their organizations. They seek out the best people in the organization for key jobs and then empower them to accomplish their goals. Their people know they care about them. It shows in everything they do. Many politicians are good leaders. Few, however, are good managers, too.

Managers possess a whole different skill set — far more quantifiable. Because most companies are striving to lower their cost structures and get their products and services to market faster, they are demanding increased technical, administrative, and financial skills from their managers. Their successful managers are not only able to see the big picture that the leaders lay out, but they can work the small functional details that are necessary to implement the vision. They understand the practical aspects of working to schedules and budgets and don't shun the administrative details of getting things done in an organization. They are conscious of time and priorities and recognize their fiduciary responsibility to their corporations.

Good managers care about their people, too, and show it by handling the administrative details of personnel actions, goal setting, performance appraisals, and development and training in a timely, consistent, and professional manner.

Attributes of Successful Leaders	Attributes of Successful Managers
Trustworthy	Fiscally Competent
Empowering	Technically Competent
Communicative	Administratively Competent
Accessible	Facilitator
Visionary	Coach
Inspirational	Able to Set Goals
Motivational	Able to Measure Performance
Able to Win Commitment	Recognizes Employees
Able to Build Loyalty	Develops Employees

So how do women stack up as managers and leaders? Author and lecturer Tom Peters often refers positively to women's leadership attributes in his newspaper columns and seminars, citing women's flexibility as an advantage to organizations. John Naisbitt and Patricia Aburdene in *Megatrends 2000* devote one-tenth of their book to discussing women in leadership. They contend that, "To be a leader in business today, it is no longer an advantage to have been socialized as a male." They also assert that, "Women may have missed out on the industrial age, but they have already established themselves in the industries of the future....Women and the information society — which celebrates brain over brawn — are a partnership made in heaven." While the book was hugely successful, these powerful statements went virtually unnoticed.

If the data support that women's skills can help corporations get where they want to go, why do companies still block women's progress? Why do the shareholders stand for it?

Published the same year, but certainly not unnoticed, was Dr. Judy B. Rosener's 1990 *Harvard Business Review* article entitled, "Ways Women Lead." Describing the article as a "lightening rod" for controversy, Dr. Rosener explains the command-and-control management style used by most men and coins the term "interactive management style" to describe the more coaching, facilitating, hands-on method preferred by most women. While she is careful to note that not all men use the command-and-control style, nor do all women use the interactive style, she finds that most men use attributes of command-and-control to describe what they view as leadership traits. In other words, command-and-control *defines* leadership for most of the men for whom women work. If this is truly their paradigm, no wonder men have a hard time seeing women as leaders, regardless of the success women have with their own styles and methods.

Dr. Rosener's research further showed that the interactive style was more effective in "flexible, nonhierarchical organizations of the kind that perform best in a climate of rapid change." While not all of our large corporations are flexible and nonhierarchical, nearly all of them claim they want to be. Read the annual reports and the press releases. Listen to the CEOs talk about how they want their companies to be "nimble," "flexible," and "more responsive to customers and changing markets." *None* of them say they want to be "large, bureaucratic, and slow moving." So, if the data support that women's skills can help corporations get where they want to go, why do companies still block women's progress? Why do the shareholders stand for it?

Data pour in from every direction. The management assessment study conducted by Lawrence Pfaff and Associates, and discussed in detail in Chapter Two, shows that women outscored men in the areas most associated with leadership: trust, self-confidence, empowerment, and accessibility. They also outscored men in areas most associated with managing the business: planning, technical expertise, coaching, and evaluating performance.

Ortho Pharmaceuticals banks savings of $500,000 per year as a result of its efforts to lower turnover among women.

Clearly, women have the skills. What needs to happen now is for the companies that have not already recognized this, to do so. In addition, *all* companies must remove the barriers that have prevented this talent from being effectively utilized. Many companies think they have human resources programs that maximize the talents and motivate *all* of their employees, but the data show that simply isn't

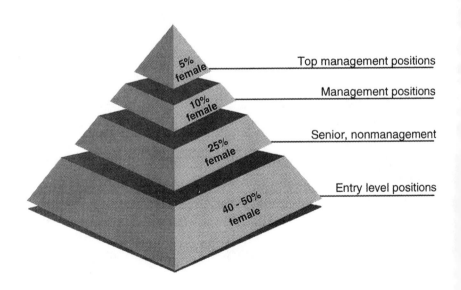

true. Felice Schwartz, president and founder of Catalyst, a national not-for-profit research and advisory organization, describes in her 1992 *Harvard Business Review* article "Women as a Business Imperative," what a typical company pyramid looks like in terms of distribution of women. While most companies start off with about half of the entry-level slots filled by women, women fall out of the ranks at the upper levels of the pyramid. At the top of the pyramid — representing senior management positions — only 3 to 5% of the slots (in a diverse company) are held by women.

So what happens? Since the feeder base for these positions has been strong for nearly 20 years, the availability of females to promote is not the issue. Rather, asserts Schwartz, companies actively do things that prevent women from reaching the tops of the pyramids. They refuse to implement policies that are female-friendly, and they allow systematic harassment and devaluation to occur unchecked. As a result, companies end up with people who are not necessarily the best at the top. They fail to maintain quality at every level of the pyramid. And they, in essence, put "a lid on the contribution individual women can make."

Schwartz's assertions are supported by findings of the federal government's Glass Ceiling Commission that identified all too common barriers to the advancement of women and minorities in U.S. corporations:

- Outreach or recruitment practices that do not seek out or reach or recruit minorities and women
- Corporate climates that alienate and isolate minorities and women
- Pipeline barriers that directly affect opportunity for advancement

  -- initial placement and clustering in jobs that are not on the career track to the top
  -- lack of mentoring

-- lack of management training
-- lack of opportunities for career development, tailored training, and rotational job assignments that are on the revenue producing side of the business
-- little or no access to critical developmental assignments such as memberships on highly visible task forces and committees
-- special or different standards for performance evaluation
-- biased rating or testing systems
-- little or no access to informal networks of communication
-- counterproductive behavior and harassment by colleagues

Considering that companies spend the same to hire and recruit a woman as a man, the fact that they inadvertently squander their investments in women through their repeated lack of awareness and insensitivity does not make good business sense. Ortho Pharmaceuticals realized this and now banks savings of $500,000 per year as a result of its efforts to lower turnover among women.

It is important for women to recognize their strengths and weaknesses. They must try to compensate for their weaknesses by building a team around them that is well-balanced and addresses all aspects of both managing and leading.

What responsibilities do women have in this scenario? Now that the data are compiled, can women just relax, confident that their skills will carry the day? Absolutely not. While women at large may stack up well in every category, it's the individual who must get ahead, and few people — men or women — possess equally strong skills of both leaders and managers. As women gain opportunity, it is important for them to recognize where their strengths and weaknesses lie and try to compensate for their weaknesses by building a team around them that is well-balanced and addresses all aspects of both managing and leading.

Hiring clones of existing team members buys nothing. It fills no gaps, and it brings no strength to the team. While it is not always comfortable to have people on our teams who see things very differently than we do, it is always necessary. Having all-female teams adds no more balance than having all-male teams. It's the blending of cultures and ideas that helps us add value and perspective to our ideas and messages.

BAD BOSSES

Sometimes, despite all screening processes in the organization, people who shouldn't be end up being bosses. Sometimes they're even yours. Learn from them.

My company had just completed a fairly large acquisition, and I was going to be managing a part of the newly acquired company. I was having a series of get-to-know-you interviews with my new direct reports. One particular person happened to be a white male who had aspects of his background that were quite similar to aspects of mine. After completing the structured part of the interview, we got off on a side conversation about expectations of bosses and subordinates and, in particular, what we liked and disliked about bosses.

This man told me about the worst boss he ever had. This boss (a man) did indeed sound bad, but I assured him I had had worse and proceeded to tell him some things about my worst boss that were really much worse than his. "Oh no," he assured me. "There was more." After a couple more rounds of "my boss from hell is worse than your boss

*from hell," we looked at each other in amazement because
we realized we were talking about the same man.*

*What was most enlightening about this discovery for me
was that I had always felt that the reason this boss was so
bad and made my two years under him the two most miserable years in my career is that he was extremely sexist
and very abusive. What I discovered from our conversation is that bad bosses are bad bosses to everybody — they
merely tailor their abuse to fit the situation.*

After this conversation, I started thinking more deliberately about
the characteristics of a "bad boss." This particular man was abusive
to his staff. He embarrassed them publicly. He berated them in front
of their peers. He blamed others for his own mistakes. He stole
credit for his subordinates' accomplishments. He denied them visibility and exposure to upper management. He dead-ended a number
of people's careers and caused many high-potential employees to leave
the company. In other words, he embodied every negative characteristic you can think of when thinking of someone for whom you don't
want to work.

So why did the company tolerate him? They didn't, for long, but
then he went to another large company in an even higher position.
He was eventually fired from there also, but he got yet another high
level executive job in yet another company. And in each company,
he left damage in his wake.

Here's another boss who wasn't entirely bad; he was just insensi-
tive:

*I received a package from my boss that contained my long-
service award. I was surprised, because the company that
furnished the awards had a catalogue from which employees could select their choice of jewelry, and I hadn't been*

DILBERT reprinted by permission of United Feature Syndicate, Inc.

75

asked to select anything. I was further chagrined at the fact that the award came in the mail. It was customary in our firm to give the awards at the quarterly awards ceremony or at least at a staff meeting. I opened the box to find my diamond studded tie tack. "Great," I thought. "This goes well with the tie I received at a sales event a couple of years before."

Between these two bosses, a list can be compiled of most of the characteristics that you do *not* want in someone for whom you work:

- Abusive to employees
- Blames others for own mistakes
- Refuses to give credit where credit is due
- Denies visibility and exposure to employees
- Does not develop employees
- Lacks integrity
- Lacks empathy
- Refuses to treat individuals individually
- Shuns employee recognition
- Poor communicator
- Uncomfortable with women or minorities
- Poor listener
- Sexist/racist

In 1992, Jim Miller, founder of BTMiller Business Systems, and author of *The Corporate Coach*, started a contest called Best Boss/ Worst Boss. At that time, the entries to the contest were about even — good bosses and bad bosses. This year, nominees for bad boss outnumbered good boss nominees by seven-to-one. With these odds, you are likely to have your own bad boss in the near term.

What if you end up with your own "boss from hell" who embodies many of these characteristics? Observe how this person interacts with others in your group. Is this a problem that only you have, or is it across the board in the organization? If it only seems to be with you, you may want to analyze why that is. Do you have a personality conflict? A style conflict? Are you being singled out for some other reason?

In the event of a style conflict with your boss, you must change *your* style.

Some women claim that they have had problems with their bosses because the women reminded them of some other woman they had conflict with — usually an ex-girlfriend or ex-wife. If the issue is one of style or some other attribute that only you possess (e.g., "You remind me of my ex-wife...."), try the following:

- Have a heart-to-heart with your boss to clear the air and re-establish a more congenial relationship.
- Be direct about the behavior that the boss exhibits that you find intolerable, but present it unemotionally, using "I" language.
- Make certain in any conversations that you are specific and are armed with examples of behavior that constitute a pattern.
- Tie every instance back into why it negatively impacts your productivity or keeps you from getting your job done, again using "I" language. ("I can't get my job done effectively when I am precluded from....")
- If the issue is one of association with someone the boss dislikes, let him or her see a different side of you — humorous, studious, athletic — so that you can break the association cycle.

If it's a matter of style only, it is incumbent upon you to adapt to fit the boss' style, because the boss is, after all, the boss. If it is more serious than that — if the problem is with the boss and *everyone*, or if the boss is abusive or unethical, you may wish to enlist the support of your human resources department or peers prior to confronting your boss. A truly abusive boss usually is very insecure or feels threatened, so it is unlikely that you can really change all that. The best bet is to communicate your feelings about the abusive behavior and the impact the behavior has on the business. Again, in extreme cases, make sure your human resources department or some viable third party is informed, if not involved.

A word of caution here. I have seen human resources departments that were very pro-employee and particularly effective, and I have seen others that were totally ineffective and did not respect confidentiality. Before revealing too much information about your problem, make sure you know whether the human resources department can really help you and will ensure confidentiality.

If they will not, try another avenue — perhaps another high ranking manager whom you do trust. It is *almost never* a good idea to go to your boss' boss if the topic of the conversation is your boss. If the higher ups didn't already support your boss, they would have put someone else in that job. By criticizing someone they support — and essentially telling them they made a bad decision — you put them in an untenable position and almost always come out the worse for it. An exception here is if your boss is committing fraud or some heinous act against the company that would most surely result in termination.

Having a bad boss is the number one stressor at the office. Don't suffer needlessly.

If it appears unlikely that you can work through the problems with your boss, ask yourself if there is anything compelling at all about working for this person:

• Is this a key job you must have to get or stay on your track?

- Is this the only time or place you can get this experience?
- Is there some key skill (other than patience) that you can learn by working with this person?

If the answer to any of these questions is yes, tough it out, try to make getting along a character-building experience, and then move on to another job as soon as possible.

If you can get the experience elsewhere or at another time, make every effort to obtain a transfer. Having a bad boss is the number one stressor at the office. Don't suffer needlessly. Explain to your boss that you would like permission to look elsewhere in the organization. If there is truly conflict between the two of you, this will probably be received as good news. If permission is not granted, enlist the support of your human resources organization. It is not uncommon for employees to want to change positions inside the company if they have bad bosses or ones with whom they've had style conflicts. Human resources should be supportive of your move if you are perceived as a valuable employee.

Whatever you do, do not bad-mouth your boss to others in your company. "Bad" is in the eye of the beholder. Others may not see this person in the same light and will only think worse of you for airing "dirty laundry." You do not want to get the reputation of being "difficult to manage" or of being a disloyal employee. Everyone can understand style conflicts. They assign no blame. Leave it at that.

GOOD BOSSES

If you get a good boss, cherish the moment and learn all you can while you can. Good bosses are few and far between.

I was trying hard to remember how many good bosses I've had out of the 20 or so bosses so far in my career. Unfortunately, it's only been three or four. Most bosses are neutral — they neither help you

79

nor hurt you, but every now and then, I've been fortunate enough to get someone who truly added value and enhanced my career.

What makes a good boss? Good bosses are bosses from whom you can learn — technically, culturally, or politically. They know more than you do in at least one of these areas and are willing to share this knowledge with you. They are willing to work with you on plotting your career path and will assist you in getting the development, assignments, and exposure necessary to stay on your path.

Good bosses value creativity and encourage their people to speak their minds. They have a vision and share that vision, as well as the information necessary to implement it, with their employees. Good bosses see themselves as the center of the organization (as a network node, if you will), rather than at the top of it. Their style is one of inclusion, rather than exclusion.

Good bosses are facilitators inside the organization who aid others in getting things done and are role models for the rest of the corporation. They act as coaches, rather than commanders, and empower their employees while working to remove barriers for them.

Reprinted by special permission of King Features Syndicate.

Really good bosses give their employees the credit when they do something right and protect their employees when they do something wrong. They are secure enough in their own careers not to worry that their subordinates may be getting recognized and promoted above them. They possess integrity, maturity, and do not in any way feel that they compete with their subordinates for visibility or recognition. They are willing to let their people do their jobs, while being there for them when they need help. They give employees honest and accurate feedback on their performance and aren't afraid to let them make mistakes. They give out work assignments, but make their people feel that the direction of their work has been arrived at jointly. This is especially important when managing knowledge workers, who often know more about their areas of expertise than their bosses and are often exasperated by attempts to micromanage them.

I was reflecting on the best boss I ever had, and what it was that singled him out. First and foremost, he was smart. This is very important to me, as I personally feel that my growth is stunted when I work for someone whom I am constantly teaching without learning something in return. I don't want patience to be the only thing I learn from my boss. This boss was focused and clear in his direction to me. I never had to go back and rework something because I didn't understand what he wanted. He didn't micromanage me. I was truly empowered. I had my assignment and was provided the authority and resources needed to carry it out.

While he was very serious about his work, he had a terrific sense of humor and wasn't afraid to show it at work. We had a pretty intense environment with a lot of long hours, including many weekends. He used humor a lot to relieve tension and boost morale. It worked. Even when he wasn't being humorous, he was upbeat and positive. Regardless of how difficult the assignments were, I had confidence our group could accomplish them under his leadership. Probably key to why I liked him so much as a boss was the fact that no matter what I did, he made me feel valuable. Even when I made mistakes, he showed me how to learn from them. He valued my contributions, and he let me and everyone else know it. I try to emulate many of the things I admired about his management and leadership style. It's been nearly 10 years since I worked for him — we've both long since changed companies — but we still keep in touch.

There are many attributes in bosses that make them great bosses for women. Look for someone who:

- Is progressive and forward thinking
- If a man, has a working wife
- If a man, has a grown daughter
- Has other women on his/her staff
- Appears to be comfortable with women at every level in the company
- Has female friends
- Socializes with women from work (even if it's just having lunch)
- Is communicative
- Recognizes employee contributions
- Admits own mistakes
- Empowers others
- Is accessible
- Recognizes the individual traits of each subordinate
- Gives clear, concise, consistent direction
- Is willing to help with your career development
- Is secure
- Has a good sense of humor

Having someone as a boss who is understanding, supportive, and comfortable with you gives you a much higher probability for advancement and job satisfaction.

Getting behind a boss who is getting ahead can do wonders for your career.

Most importantly, a good boss for anyone who is serious about getting ahead is a boss who is getting ahead. An upwardly mobile boss is usually a good role model and someone with whom you want to be associated. Furthermore, being behind someone who is moving forward provides much more opportunity than being behind someone who is "dead in place." And someone who is moving will not resent *you* and your plans to move ahead.

When you have the privilege of working for the kind of bosses described above, watch how they operate. Learn from their actions and words. If your boss doesn't exhibit these characteristics, look around the organization for one who does, and use this person as your role model. The way you will learn to be a good boss is to observe positive behaviors in others and adapt those behaviors to fit your style.

Observing and learning from others in order to build your own "good boss" portfolio is essential because in order for you to get ahead in business, you must be perceived as a good boss. Just as your manager can inhibit or promote your career, so can your employees — you succeed or fail through their performance. If you have a reputation for being a good boss, good people will want to join you. You will be able to attract the best and brightest, build a strong team, and perform in a manner that will get you noticed. Never forget that you succeed through others. The better the "others" are whom you can attract to your team, the more successful you will be.

The next chapter discusses the important subject of managing your boss — good or bad.

Chapter Five

Managing Up

> *Be kind to everyone; they might*
> *end up being your boss someday.*
>
> -Maxine Kiely

GETTING ALONG

Treat your boss as you would any other important customer.

Regardless of what kind of boss you have at any point in your career, there are several things you should remember. First and foremost, accept that you have a boss. Nearly everyone has one, but for many reasons, some people have trouble acknowledging it. It is particularly difficult for people to accept bosses who they believe do not add value or are unworthy of the position. One woman tells her story:

> *I was fairly new with the company — about a year. The*
> *man who hired me and who I had hoped would mentor me*
> *retired shortly after I joined the company. Another man*

was brought in to be my boss. During my first year, I had a series of short-term assignments, one of which was to develop a market and technology strategy for our new division. I completed the strategy and presented it on viewgraphs to several people at the corporate strategy office. Meanwhile, my new boss came in. I was shocked when I read his resume. He had a fraction of my experience and credentials. He immediately assigned me to something I thought was meaningless, but I was determined to give the assignment my best effort. Meanwhile, he said he would continue on with my strategy effort personally, as he had a deadline from his boss. I watched from the sidelines while he brought in consultant after consultant and spent tens of thousands of dollars.

Finally, the big day arrived when he was going to "roll out the strategy." He rented a ballroom at a nearby hotel for the entire division. Everyone showed up, anxious to see the direction in which we would be heading. I, especially, was curious, since he took what I considered to be my completed work, added four months of effort and thousands of dollars to it, and never discussed it with me again. What did he do with all that money? The presentation was excellent. The strategy was well-received. Afterwards, the man who headed up the corporate strategy office came over to me with a smirk on his face. We both knew what he was thinking. My new boss had spent all that time and all that money and had merely converted my viewgraph presentation to 35mm slides. I got no credit. The only people who knew were at the corporate office. Later, my boss got a big promotion, and this "strategy effort" was cited as one of the main reasons.

Regardless of how you feel about your boss' contribution, your boss is still the boss and is one of your most important internal customers. The quality of your work and your communications with your boss must be topnotch. You absolutely want this person to believe that he or she can give you any assignment, walk away from it, and trust that, upon return, it will have been performed flawlessly.

The more senior you are in the organization, the more important your relationship with your boss becomes.

Get along with your boss. This may be difficult, especially if you have conflicting styles. In the event that you do, it is *your* responsibility to alter your style to be in less conflict with the boss' and to tailor your work to meet his or her needs. For instance, if you have a boss who is a data sponge, always have plenty of data available in the format and form the boss finds acceptable. If the boss is a "net it out" kind of person, make sure you are brief, to the point, and always have everything tightly summarized.

This may take some practice, but understanding the boss' style and preferences upfront will save lots of wasted time and effort in the long run and will leave the boss with a more favorable impression of you and your work.

The more senior you are in the organization, the more important your relationship with your boss becomes. At the uppermost levels, many executives fail simply because they do not get along well or do not see eye-to-eye with their bosses. We can all name many competent professionals who lost their positions or ended their careers simply because they refused to take the actions required to get along. Most of the cabinet-level political appointees who left their positions prematurely during the last several administrations did so because they lost favor with the president. Had they made the effort that many times calls for subjugating their own egos, they might have survived.

If you are having problems with your boss, first determine if it is your fault. Are you being insubordinate? Hostile? Fighting direction? Fostering an antagonistic relationship with your boss will not only hinder you from getting plum assignments, it will hinder your movement and visibility in the corporation. Getting along is *your* responsibility.

Perhaps you don't really *not* get along, you just don't "connect." Women usually excel at building relationships because they spend their whole lives trying to connect with others and are usually willing to change their styles, suppress their egos, or do anything else needed to form a "bond." Women are usually more direct when they perceive a problem and more willing to talk it through to its resolution. The drawback for women, however, is that many women who usually are good at bonding with others have trouble bonding or connecting with male bosses. This is usually based on the fact that both the women and the men believe they have little in common outside of work. While the men at the office can huddle around the coffee pot and discuss last night's sports scores or tomorrow's big golf game, most women feel out of place joining in these conversations.

I encourage women to search for common ground. Read the sports section or at least watch the three minute sports recap on the morning news. Have some level of awareness of the things that interest your boss. Look for commonality in other areas as well — children of similar ages, vacation spots you particularly like, the pitfalls of being a homeowner — anything that will give you something on which to build some kind of rapport. Invite your boss to lunch. Try to personalize your relationship.

A big challenge here for a woman is if she works for a male boss who is simply not comfortable with women in the workplace. If this is your situation, it is your responsibility to try to connect enough with the boss for him to be comfortable, but recognize that you may be able to make only small steps of progress. In all cases, make certain that nothing about your work can be criticized or challenged — that your outputs are all flawless.

BEING A TEAM PLAYER

Know how your boss is measured and make sure that your actions and results support those goals.

It is important that your boss see you as a team player — one who is supportive of the group's goals, in general, and his or her goals, in particular. In trying to support your boss' and the team's goals, make sure you understand what they are. If they are not published or are not flowed down to you as your own goals, ask about them. Read the chairman's statement in the annual report, the organization's strategic plan, the operating plan, and any other documents that contain mission statements or direction.

Determine how your boss is measured and make certain that you understand the priorities so that you can effectively make trade-off decisions during the course of the year. Knowing whether revenue or profit or cash flow is more important, for example, can have a profound impact on your negotiations with clients and suppliers. Knowing what your boss and the rest of senior management consider truly important should help you set your own priorities and manage your time, as well as let you know what can "fall off the plate," in the event that you — like everyone else — simply cannot do it all.

When problems arise for your boss, be part of the solution, not the problem. Do an excellent job, and be willing to help out in areas outside your purview to support the group's goals. If there is a major project in the company that is in trouble, volunteer resources to help out. Sometimes this may mean giving up key resources for a period of time, but being a team player means sharing in the pain when the group has a problem.

Women seem to support others especially well because this typically entails thinking outside the box and juggling multiple resources — skills they have honed over the years in managing multiple tasks and priorities around the household and inside the family unit. Where women generally fall short, however, is in the area of getting credit. If the opportunity to "donate" occurs, give all you can. Just make sure others recognize your contribution. Altruism is not career-enhancing.

Don't dump problems on your boss' desk. Think through the problems and have multiple solutions available.

Bring your boss solutions, not more problems. Never, *ever*, bring your boss a problem without having worked through possible solutions. If it is *your* project that is in trouble, come to your boss with a plan to fix it. Know what resources you need from other parts of the company and how long you will need them. Know how much you will overrun your budget and what impact it will have on the bottom line.

It is acceptable to ask for guidance on which solution to use or how to go about finding the solutions, but do not just drop problems on your boss' desk. If your boss has to solve all the problems herself, why pay you?

Women who work for men should be aware of the differences in the way men and women solve problems. Women typically talk the problem through and brainstorm solutions before acting. Men typically make a decision quickly and immediately act upon it. Be cognizant of the fact that if you attempt to talk the problem through with your male boss before you solve it, he may well think you are asking him to solve it for you.

There are numerous stories about male doctors, lawyers, or information workers who managed women and thought the women were less competent than their male counterparts because the women asked more questions or wanted to discuss different solutions. Men who are not aware of the differences in the ways women communicate compare everything women do to how *they* would do it. Most men will not ask their bosses for clarification on a point, to brainstorm solutions, or to discuss a problem with them. In their minds this constitutes a lack of strength or knowledge on their part. Therefore, when women do it, that's exactly the presumption that they have about women. Be aware of this and balance your need for information with your need to appear confident and competent.

Think "big picture." You cannot make leaps in your career if you think parochially.

People who are very successful in business are able to think "big picture." Even if they have specific goals pertaining only to their areas, they are able to meet those goals while looking out for the greater good of the corporation. This is all part of being "on the team."

You cannot make leaps in your career if you are small-minded and think parochially. Understand the company's mission, as well as the mission of your division and your own organization. Know how your part fits into the total picture, and make sure you do all the right things to make the company successful.

Loyalty — to your boss, to your company — is important. One might ask how — in today's environment of massive downsizing and layoffs — one can be loyal to an employer when you well know that when times are hard, all bets are off. Very simply, while you work for a company and a boss, and you accept their pay, you owe them loyalty. You may decide that, for whatever reason, you need to leave their employ; but while you are still there, you must be loyal to the company's goals and your boss' direction.

Be supportive of the goals of the organization in general and your boss in particular. When you feel you must, you may disagree privately, one-on-one with your boss, but never in a group unless the group has been asked specifically to critique an idea or action.

When you disagree with your boss — and you will — make sure the disagreement is private, assertive, and factual. Sometimes your boss will not accept your recommendations, and you may feel strongly that the company will suffer as a result. Try to enlist peer support. Often if the boss hears it from more than one party, it will have greater impact. If this still doesn't work, try another angle — perhaps a peer of your boss whom you trust.

While you accept the company's money, you must be loyal to its mission.

When you disagree privately, be courteous and factual about why you believe something is a bad idea. Base the argument on sound business considerations, avoiding personal opinion or emotion. Try to change the boss' mind, but if you are unable to do so, accept defeat and publicly support the boss' direction. You're walking a fine line here.

> *Early on in my career, my boss had made a decision that I was sure would result in disaster. I believed I had made a valiant attempt to change his mind in a private meeting. He did not accept my recommendations and went forward with his plan. Sure enough, disaster ensued. Afterwards, he came storming into my office and asked me if I had known that things would turn out so disastrously. I assured him I had and referenced our prior conversation. His response was that I hadn't persevered enough and brought him enough supporting facts to make him understand why I might be right. He felt that it was my job to keep him out of trouble, and I had failed to do so.*

If the consequences to the company are severe, do not give up. If you hold information that could prevent a disaster with a client or could limit the company's liability, do not keep it to yourself. If your boss blocks the information flow and you do not take action to find an alternative path, you have become part of the problem. As a last resort, bring your boss' boss into the loop, but try to do it in a non-threatening way. Perhaps send your boss a memo with a copy to her boss. Don't drop the ball. Here's the perspective from up the chain when information is withheld:

I was managing a large organization that developed custom software. We had over 50 clients — and we were developing over 20 systems for one particular client. Needless to say, I couldn't personally keep my hands on everything that was going on all the time. I was well aware of this and felt that I, along with my management staff, fostered an environment of openness and trust. I encouraged the use of an open door policy and met personally with a number of the people at all levels in the organization.

The software we were developing for this particular client was of concern to me, partly because there was so much of it, and partly because the client's requirements weren't clear. I had directed my operations director to have weekly review meetings of this software development effort in order to ensure that if anything got off track, we could fix it before there was an impact on the business. Things were going well, we were making every deliverable to the client, and everyone seemed to be happy.

I had instituted a monthly breakfast meeting with a few of the employees from different levels of the organization in order to maintain some contact and visibility into the things that were going on in the organization. One of the regular attendees was the senior developer on this project. I'll call him "John." We met often and talked at length. He seemed excited about his job and assured me that everything was going well.

A few weeks later, we were barraged with a series of facsimiles from this client complaining about the quality and timeliness of our deliverables. This was severe enough for my boss to get involved. He and I discussed the severity of the complaints and decided rather than just try to answer them one at a time, we would do an internal audit on the program and see if the problems were real or perceived and how severe they really were.

They were real. They were severe. And they were not new. Apparently, they had been present for some time and had been raised by "John" repeatedly to his boss. However, his boss refused to fix them and never raised them further. I was John's boss' boss' boss and I saw him regularly. He never let on that there was a problem. He eventually quit the company in frustration — at about the same time the problem was raised by the customer.

As a result of John's refusal to go around his boss, the company lost a great deal of money on something that easily could have been fixed. John's boss got taken out of his job, and we lost credibility with the client. I was furious with John's boss, but I was even more angry with John. He was closest to the problem, and he had ample opportunity to see that it got raised above his boss. His refusal to own the problem cost us all far more than if he had just gone around his boss — an act that I believe would have been the only responsible thing to do.

Because most women have *not* grown up in rigid command-and-control environments, they find it easier to work both within and outside the chain-of-command. When one path is blocked, most women easily find another avenue for information flow. Where women need to be cautious is when they have people in their chain-of-command who are inflexible or are threatened by a break in the chain. It is important to work inside the structure whenever possible, keep your boss informed, and go outside the structure only when not doing so would be detrimental to the company's best interest.

MANAGING EXPECTATIONS

A key part of managing your boss is setting up realistic expectations and then meeting or exceeding them.

In most companies, success is measured in large part by the ability to set realistic expectations or goals and meet or exceed all of them. Make sure your boss knows what is possible as well as what is impossible. Making promises you cannot fulfill is a path to disaster. Always assume that your plans are part of the big picture and that your actions, good and bad, impact others. When you think this way, it is easy to see how a minor error in planning or a shortfall of your goals can blossom into a major embarrassment for your boss.

One man for whom I used to work was unbelievably successful. It seemed like every year he was getting another promotion. I observed this man carefully to see what it was that made him so extraordinary. He was smart, but not brilliant. He had good presence, but was not the most charismatic person I'd worked with. I talked to several people who had known him for a number of years. They all said the same thing. He had never missed his operating plan. He always made his goals. In more than 20 years, he had never missed his objectives. But they also all said this — his strength was in setting a plan he could always make. He was a master at negotiating his goals every year. It worked. He had figured out early on that it was much better to accept a conservative plan he could always make than to take a "stretch" plan that he had a chance of missing. He never let his ego get in the way of his common sense.

95

Most people are judged not on whether they make mistakes, but on how they correct the ones they do make.

Never surprise your boss. Always keep the boss informed, especially if you have changed actions or plans or have made a mistake that will impact others. It's best to own up to it and be the one to tell the boss yourself. No one who has managed people for any length of time expects their employees to be perfect. It just isn't possible. Most people are judged not on whether they make mistakes, but on how they correct the ones they do make. Take responsibility for your mistakes, as well as for concrete actions to fix them.

Most women don't seem to have much of a problem with admitting a mistake or asking for help when they get into trouble. For the most part, they've been socialized to be part of a team and to be unafraid to ask for help or support. Again, though, here is an area where women can get into trouble with their openness and directness. Many women are so open and direct about their mistakes and shortcomings, that they appear less competent or confident than they really are. There is a difference between keeping your boss informed of problems and highlighting weaknesses unnecessarily. Share what is necessary to enhance the success of the business, but don't degrade your image of competence without cause.

GETTING REVIEWED

Don't count on someone else's memory to get credit for all that you have accomplished. Manage your own review.

Most of us receive written performance appraisals from our managers at least once a year. This is a great opportunity to accomplish several things. First and foremost, use this opportunity to ensure that your boss knows what you have accomplished during the year. It is difficult for anyone to know all of the things every employee does all year, especially if the manager has a large staff. Don't count on someone else's memory to credit you for all you have done. Use a "review checklist," such as the one below, to ensure that you are well-prepared for your next review and to maximize the impact:

- Document events as they occur, even if you just write them down on a piece of paper that you keep in your desk drawer.
- Prior to review time, write events down in a coherent manner for your boss. Cite your strengths and accomplishments.
- Quantify your accomplishments when you can. How much revenue were you responsible for? Did you affect cost savings? Did you add new customers?
- Compare accomplishments to the goals that you set forth at the beginning of the year. Present them to your boss with a plan for how to continue them into the following year.
- Attach any supporting data available from internal and external customers praising your support or accomplishments.
- Make a list of the things you have done to improve your competency during the year. Did you complete a degree? Participate in a task force? Attend a seminar? Read 10 business or technical books?
- Make this comprehensive package available *before* your boss has to write your review, not afterward. Chances are, others have already seen the review by the time it is delivered to you, and it is a *fait accompli* by the time you see it.

During your performance appraisal is a good time to discuss where you are in your career plan and how you would like your manager's support for training, development, and gaining that next key assignment. Make sure you clearly communicate your goals for the next review period, as well as your long-term career goals. Test the waters as to how realistic your goals are and determine how much support you can expect. If your manager does not support your goals or the development you feel you need, probe to find out why not. Is it performance related? Is it personal? Perhaps your goals were not realistic? Try to work through the issues and get honest feedback so that you can put together a workable and supportable plan.

If you cannot negotiate an acceptable career plan and level of support with your manager, it may be time for you to change bosses.

If your manager chooses to give you negative feedback during this review, do not be offended, defensive, or argumentative. Be thankful. Most managers are not that forthcoming and courageous, and many dread reviews altogether. Listen carefully to what he or she is saying. Ask for specific instances where you need improvement, and *how* you might go about improving. You may not agree with the feedback, but it is valuable because it tells you how you are perceived by at least one person in the company. Chances are, others see you that way as well. If you are intent on getting ahead, it is extremely important to know how you are viewed, so *never* discourage feedback along those lines.

Make your review a positive experience by being prepared, honest, and open. Try earnestly to learn more about your strengths and weaknesses, and test the waters for the level of support you can expect from your manager.

THE "MANAGING UP" CHECKLIST

Periodically review the following checklist and assure yourself that you are doing everything you can to manage your boss effectively:

- Get along with your boss.
- Adapt to a style not in conflict with your boss' style, if necessary.
- Perform well in your assignments.
- Solve your own problems.
- Keep your boss out of trouble.

- Provide data to your boss in the quantity, style, and format desired.
- Set realistic expectations and deliver on them.
- Be publicly supportive of your boss' goals.
- Never surprise your boss.
- Get credit for your accomplishments by managing your own review.

Add your own specifics to this list to cover unique aspects of your job or assignment. If you can manage to this list, and your work is above reproach, your boss will view you as someone who is reliable, dependable, and supportive. He or she will be more likely to support you in your career goals and aspirations and to help you obtain the developmental opportunities and key assignments that will move you toward the top.

The next chapter deals with when *you* are the boss.

Chapter Six

Managing Down

> *The best executive is the one who has sense*
> *enough to pick good (wo)men to do what*
> *(s)he wants done, and self-restraint enough*
> *to keep from meddling with them while they do it.*

-Teddy Roosevelt

MANAGING PEOPLE *IS* YOUR JOB

Managing down includes doing all the things a good boss does and none of the things a bad boss does.

A key part of managing is dealing with the personnel aspects of your job. New managers often miss the point that as a manager of people, the people *are* your job. It is your job to communicate with them, develop them, assign work to them, and evaluate their work. Your employees should never feel that managing them is a burden or that it is taking time away from your "real work." Being accessible to your people is a must — visits by members of your staff should never be treated as interruptions. Your job is to be there for them and to help remove barriers that prevent them from reaching their maximum productivity. If you do this job well, your employees will help ensure your success. Management studies have shown that women score high on accessibility to employees, regardless of the level of the woman. Most women just naturally want to connect with their employees and are able to leverage this as a management strength.

Good managers are able to delegate all of the workload out to their staffs and then spend their time on the personnel aspects of the business and on those parts requiring intergroup cooperation, internal interfacing, and working with clients. Delegating is difficult for many people, especially for managers who became managers because they were the best, technically, in their groups. It is difficult to let someone do something when you know you would do it better yourself, but it is the only way that they will learn — and that you can be free to handle higher-level issues.

In personnel matters, focus on the issue, not the person, and document everything.

Over time, as personnel matters arise, deal with them effectively and immediately. Do not let them fester because chances are they will only get worse. Make sure that when the problems are severe, your boss is informed at all times.

For many people, knowing what to do with personnel matters is very different from actually doing it. Telling an employee that he or she is doing something wrong can be uncomfortable. Key points to remember are:

- Always maintain the employee's self-esteem by focusing on the behavior at issue, and not the person.
- Focus on the issue at hand and don't allow the conversation to veer off onto other topics.

102

- Be specific.
- Tell the employee why the issue is important to him/her and to the organization.
- Give the employee time to respond, and actively listen to the response.
- Avoid personal attacks.
- Avoid emotion.
- Work with the employee, offering suggestions, not commands, so that a way can be found to resolve the situation.
- Summarize the conclusions at the end of the conversation and give the employee a chance to show comprehension.

This sounds difficult, and it often is, especially when one or both of you is emotional. Thorough preparation, including a mental rehearsal of possible responses from the employee, is helpful. In particularly sticky situations, some people will even role play with their human resources professional or manager prior to delivering the news or having the discussion with the employee. Following these guidelines can diffuse the tension and keep the conversation focused on resolving the problem. One woman tells how she used these guidelines very effectively:

> *I once had an employee whose personal problems had so impacted work that I had to send him home from an extended out-of-town assignment. I invited his immediate supervisor to sit in on the discussion. The employee became very emotional. While I honored his feelings, I kept returning to the situation and the impact on the organization. We were able to complete the discussion with his buy-in to the idea of going home. Afterward, his supervisor expressed her amazement at how well the conversation went. A few years later, I ran into the employee. He had left the company and was now a client. He asked to speak to me privately. He said he wanted to tell me that he understood the steps I had taken and was appreciative of*

the sensitivity I had shown to his situation. My response to this highly sensitive situation served as a model for my managers to emulate and as a relationship builder that assisted me in dealing with him as a client long after the event occurred.

Chances are, if you ever have to fire or lay off a significant number of people, you will be sued. Following all policies and procedures and documenting the process extensively will allow your company to defend you adequately.

In all personnel situations, document everything. Chances are, if you work in a large company, manage large numbers of people, and you ever have to fire or lay off a significant number of them, you will be sued. Following all policies and procedures and documenting the process extensively will allow your company to defend you adequately.

When taking drastic steps, like firing someone, make sure your boss understands what you are doing, why, and when, and will support your action even if the situation becomes uncomfortable later.

> *Once when I was put in a new assignment, I discovered that I had serious personnel problems with a senior manager. He had performance problems, sexual harassment problems, racial harassment problems, client problems, conflict of interest problems, and so many others, it took two pages to list them all. I discussed this with my boss and told him I believed this employee should be terminated immediately, considering the liability his actions created for the company, compounded by the fact that he was also pilfering money from his department. My boss agreed, and I began working with the human resources department to handle this.*

Because of the severity of the situation and the fact that it involved ethics violations and fraud, we were able to terminate his employment very quickly. Much to my surprise, my boss was very upset and called me to ask "what in heaven's name" had happened. When I reviewed our conversation with him, he remembered all the things we had discussed, including the part about firing him. "Of course, I agreed with you," he said. "I just never thought you'd actually fire him!" I later went through several anxious weeks while we were receiving letters from the man's lawyers, waiting to see if he would file suit — never knowing if my boss would support me if he did.

HIRING AND DEVELOPING PEOPLE

Because it is your people who will, in large part, determine your success, hiring and developing them will be key to getting ahead.

Hiring and developing employees is an essential part of "managing down." It is your people, after all, who will in large part determine your success or failure. A successful manager will strive to surround herself with people who complement her strengths and meet the full range of skills needed to execute the job. *By having excellent people in key jobs, your success is virtually ensured.* In building a team or filling vacancies, it is wise to assess and understand exactly what kind of people you're looking for. The more specifically the personnel requirements can be defined, the more likely good candidates can be found. The more care that is taken in screening candidates, assessing and verifying credentials, and getting to know candidates through personal interaction, the more likely a good employee will be selected.

The importance of the interviewing and hiring process goes beyond the selection of good people. It is an opportunity to showcase your judgment and style. Your management and human resources representatives notice the outcome of your interviews and the impact of your hiring decisions on the organization. Moreover, the process provides an opportunity to meet and impress new people. A positive impression left with a job candidate will be remembered by the candidate. Even if the candidate doesn't come to work for you now, that person may become a proponent of yours in the future.

When interviewing candidates, solid preparation is important. Having a list of questions ready and taking time to study the applicant's resume are steps successful managers take to prepare. As important as being ready to ask questions of the candidate is being prepared to discuss your company, organization, management style and expectations, and the role you envision for the candidate. The interview is a two-way discussion. While you're deciding if the candidate is a good fit for you, the candidate is deciding if she is a good fit for your company, and specifically, if she wants to work for you. As much as the candidate is selling herself, you must sell your company as a place to work and yourself as a boss.

With these preliminaries out of the way, you can devote your time in the interviews to getting to know the candidates better, understanding their interest in your company, their work ethics, how they will fit in with your team, and all of the seemingly intangible things that can make or break a long-term relationship between the employee and the company. I usually make up a score sheet for candidates in interviews, and score them on a number of areas such as technical competence, relevant experience, interpersonal skills, willingness to work as part of a team, and other factors that are germane to the position I'm trying to fill. I then focus on the soft requirements, using intuition and gut feeling to score the candidate's style and the likelihood that the person will fit into our corporate culture and, specifically, into my organization. I use the score sheets to compare candidates.

If I am interviewing several candidates, I usually bring the top two or three in for second interviews before I narrow my selection to the final candidate. If the position for which I am recruiting has a management or interface component to it, I will often have peers interview the candidate as well. Some of the things I have seen done in interviewing that I think should be avoided include:

- Having the subordinates interview their future boss
- Having "group gropes" or panel interviews where multiple people interview the candidate simultaneously
- When the interviewer talks too much and listens too little
- When the interviewer is unprepared and seems to be reading the candidate's resume for the first time during the interview
- When there are multiple interviewers and they have not co-ordinated what they will each tell the candidate about the organization and company
- When the interviewer asks irrelevant questions like, "What should your tombstone say?" or, "If you were a tree, what kind of a tree would you be?"
- When the interviewer is late and keeps the candidate waiting
- When the interviewer can't make up her mind and brings the candidate in more than three times

After making sure I'm completely comfortable with the candidate, have verified all credentials, and have checked all references, I try to move quickly to make an offer. Throughout the process I am careful to keep any commitments I make to keep the candidate informed of progress or provide follow-up information. The goal is to leave the candidate feeling positive about me and my company, regardless of whether I decide to bring the person on board.

A word of caution about checking references. Don't count on someone else to do that for you. While most human resources departments tell you they handle that, here is a real-world story that tells that they often do not, even when they say they do:

We had recently hired a person from outside the company to head up a department that worked closely with mine. While I was not asked to interview her during the interview process, I was given her resume to review. After she was hired, she seemed to be having an inordinate amount of trouble with her job, especially considering her credentials. Her resume stated that she had won numerous top sales awards, had held key positions with two of our competitors — one job similar to the one she was in now for us — and that she had a technical undergraduate degree followed by a Harvard MBA. It happened that I was close friends with a senior executive at one of the companies she listed on her resume.

One night, my friend and I were having dinner and I asked if he knew her. He did, indeed, as she used to work in his organization. He then asked me how she was working out. Not wanting to speak ill of her, I shrugged off the question and said, "Well, I guess it's going to take a little time for her to get used to the company." He then startled me by saying, "I'm surprised your company hired her for such a strategic job, considering her background." "What do you mean?" I queried. "Well, we fired her for nonperformance, and that was after she'd been fired from her previous job. The only reason we hired her was because I play tennis with her husband and did it as a favor to him with the understanding that if she didn't work out, we'd fire her, too." "But what about her sales awards?" "She's never won any sales awards. She's never made quota."

Feeling at this point like I had to defend my company's decision to hire her, I said, "Well at least she has her MBA from Harvard. That ought to be worth something." At this point, my friend, a Harvard man himself, burst into laughter. "Why, she doesn't even have a degree. She's working on it at night at the community college. It looks like you got taken!" Indeed we did, as this woman had

*commanded an extraordinarily high salary. Her boss had
justified it based on a set of what appeared to be impec-
cable credentials — all "verified" by human resources staff
members.*

**Sometimes you hire the wrong people. Admit it and take action
immediately. This will not get better with time.**

Sometimes, despite your best efforts, you will make hiring mistakes. Perhaps the candidate misrepresented certain strengths, or you
failed to ask the right questions. For whatever reason, admit the
mistake as soon as it is apparent, and take action. Many companies
have a 90-day "probationary" period in which a new employee can
be dismissed with few questions asked and little chance of litigation.

If you discover your mistake outside this window, fast action is
still required. The action may be to:

- Find a way for the employee to succeed in your organization
  through training or development.
- Identify another assignment in the company where the indi-
  vidual has a good chance to succeed.
- Initiate monitored performance or other corrective action.
- Initiate the firing process.

Once again, the actions you take to correct the situation will be
recognized by your management. If you can find a way to make the
employee successful, it will increase your stature as a problem solver
and leader. If you plan to move the person to another part of the
company, be careful not simply to saddle another manager with a
problem. That manager will be sure to remember and return the "favor." If punitive action is needed, the better you are able to execute
the actions without placing the company at risk or lowering morale,

the more successful you will be perceived by management, your peers, and your staff.

When you are searching for candidates, consider a multitude of sources. Internal employees often can give excellent referrals, as can friends and competitors. Running ads and surfing the Internet can yield interesting resumes in a variety of areas. For key jobs, especially at the more senior level, recruiters often play a big part. They have huge networks of contacts, work confidentially, and usually do careful screening. Their fees may be hefty, so it needs to be a position you are willing to pay a considerable amount to fill. Using more than one source for a particular position will provide a wider variety of candidates and will increase your chances of finding the "right" one.

Once employees are on board, it is your responsibility as the manager to make sure that they have the development and skill training necessary to stay current in their jobs and eventually to grow beyond where they were when they joined your organization. Development may mean training, education, experience, reading, or mentoring. Some of the most important development is experiential. Many people learn more from task forces or special projects that require them to stretch and think in new and innovative ways than they will ever learn from a class. If you are in a high-technology industry, be aware of the fact that *your industry knowledge will become obsolete every six years.* It is essential that you provide an environment of continuous learning for yourself and the people in your organization.

Your role as a manager is to be an opportunity provider to your employees.

Whatever development your employees need, make sure you are aware of it. In helping the employee develop, it is critical that your role is that of opportunity provider. This means:

- Providing honest feedback regarding developmental needs
- Assisting in defining what is available and possible
- Approving the employee for training
- Being supportive of the employee's efforts

It is the employee's job to determine the specific actions he or she wishes to pursue. By allowing employees to take ownership of their development, you empower them and increase their likelihood of success. Moreover, it will increase your credibility as a manager who builds strong teams of qualified, motivated employees.

PROMOTING FROM WITHIN

Employees must see some movement inside the company or they will come to believe there is no opportunity for them.

If every job opening is filled from the outside, employees become demoralized and feel that they have no career path. Part of the employee development task of every manager is cross-training and upward mobility. Employees should never be left in one job too long. It makes them stale, and they stop being creative and excited about their jobs.

I once took over an organization in which one of the employees had been in his same job for 29 years! I wanted to move him but he was ready to retire. Imagine, his entire career in the same job with the same customer! My rule of thumb for knowledge workers in the high-tech industry is that employees should not be in junior-level jobs more than two years, and mid-level jobs more than three or four. Even if the employee is not ready to be promoted, she should be given a lateral transfer, or a new customer or product to work on. When employees are bored or demoralized, their creativity and productivity take a dive.

Other reasons to hire or promote from within include:

- **It's free.** It requires no advertising or recruiting fees.
- **It's motivational.** Other employees always find out about an internal promotion and feel good about the prospects of advancement for them.
- **It has a domino effect.** Usually, when someone moves up, it creates opportunities for others.
- **It's productive.** When you hire someone from inside the company, you avoid the learning curve associated with building a network and adjusting to a new culture that you have with outside hires.
- **It's good advertising for you.** Word gets around. If employees believe you create opportunities for them, good employees will want to be a part of your team.

I always try to hire or promote from within first. I go outside only if I absolutely cannot get the skills I need from inside the company.

REVIEWING PERFORMANCE

Most people hate performance appraisals, whether they are giving them or getting them. Some planning and a checklist can make them less painful for all involved.

Most managers hate performance appraisals. They hate writing them, they hate giving them, and they hate all the paperwork involved in tracking them. Many managers do not keep notes on their employees during the year so it's a mad scramble at the end of the year to try to remember enough things the employee did all year to write an effective appraisal. Most of us are somewhat conflict-avoidant, so it's difficult for us to give employees any negative feedback about their performance — even though this is the kind from which people learn. Women seem to be more willing than men to give open, honest feedback to employees, no matter how difficult the news is. Here are a few pointers that will make performance appraisal time less painful for all parties involved:

- Give all employees written goals at the beginning of the year and explain to them how the goals will be measured. Will they all have equal weight? What if a goal is partially fulfilled?
- Keep a file on each employee and drop notes or memos into it all year that will jog your memory at review time about what key things they accomplished.
- Drop into this same file a copy of any recognition awards or customer appreciation notes the employee receives during the year.
- Give the employee constant feedback during the year so that there are no surprises at review time.
- Have one informal, interim review halfway through the year in which you and the employee pull out the employee's goals and discuss progress toward them.
- When it is a few weeks prior to review time, give the employees copies of their goals and ask for their input on their accomplishments toward them. No matter how good your notes, you will leave something out that the employee will consider crucial to a fair review.
- Take your employee file that you have been keeping, combined with the employee input, and complete the review form, making every effort to be thorough and accurate.
- Make sure that you are consistent across employee reviews. If you use third person on one, use it on all. If you use first names on one, use them on all.

- Schedule an appointment for the review so that you will have a period of uninterrupted quality time, and you will not be rushed.
- When delivering the reviews, make sure you explain your methodology to the employees so that they understand how thorough and fair you have attempted to be.
- Stick to the employees' performance against their goals. Review time is not the time to start changing what you wanted them to do for the last year.
- Make positive feedback specific. Give examples of things the employee did that were exceptional. Use the customer appreciation letters or recognition awards you have collected in the file as references here.
- Make negative feedback specific. Be prepared to give examples of why the employee's performance was not up to par. Don't just say, "You miss deadlines." Say, "You were three days late on the Alexander proposal and two weeks late on your budget inputs." Suggest ways the employee might improve. "I believe you tried to do too much on the Alexander proposal by yourself. We made resources available to you to use, and you didn't take advantage of them. You might have been able to stay on schedule if you had delegated more."
- Avoid discussions of personality, unless it is directly impacting the employee's performance.
- Listen when it is the employee's turn to talk.
- Ask employees if they believe *you* can do anything to help them be more effective in their jobs and increase their performance.
- Wrap up with a summary of what you told the employee and what you heard as feedback. Include a summary of any actions you agreed to as a result of the review.
- Agree on how and when the next year's goals will be set and measured.

- Be sensitive to the fact that this is probably uncomfortable for all but a very few employees.

With some planning and some sensitivity, appraisal time can be a productive and rewarding time for you to give employees valuable feedback, learn more about your role in removing barriers for them, discuss career opportunities, and get them re-energized to meet the next year's goals.

MOTIVATING, RECOGNIZING, AND OTHER MANAGEMENT TIDBITS

Understanding what combination and proportion of factors motivates each of your direct reports will allow you to keep them happy and motivated.

All people are motivated differently, but I've found that most people are motivated by some combination of the following:

- **Money.** Be it salary, commissions, or bonuses, some people are happy to work in a broom closet and have no title and no real perks, as long as they make plenty of money. Most salespeople are in this category.
- **Power/Prestige.** Some people are motivated by how big of a budget they control, how many people work for them, what kinds of decisions they make, and the impact they have on the company's bottom line. They care about titles and where they fall on the organization chart. Usually, these people are already at fairly high levels and make quite comfortable salaries.
- **Perks/Benefits.** Many people really do care what kind of office they have and whether they get a company car. Others care whether they get club memberships and additional life

insurance. While many of these things seem intangible to some people, they are very tangible to this group.

- **Job flexibility.** Rather than living to work, the people who "work to live" are very motivated by job flexibility. The ability to telecommute, have flextime, or take time off for key events in their children's lives is very important to this group of workers.

- **Intellectual stimulation.** Some people can make lots of money and have lots of power and perks but will not be happy if their job is not intellectually stimulating. They need to be continually challenged and constantly on-the-go at work.

Managers should understand the individual characteristics of the people they manage, and treat the people individually. Understanding what combination and proportion of factors motivates each of your direct reports will allow you to keep them happy and motivated. If you have decisions to make with respect to office space, tickets to conferences, training classes, and time off, knowing how important — or unimportant — these things are to your employees will allow you to make balanced decisions that motivate, rather than demotivate.

Most people who quit their jobs do so because they don't believe that their accomplishments are recognized. The cost of recognition is significantly less than the cost of rehiring and training.

Recognition, while not included in the list above, is also a key motivator for many people, especially those who are not on a bonus or commission plan. When employees do something out of the ordinary, whether it's working extra-long hours on a client presentation or proposal or agreeing at the drop of a hat to take a temporary assignment for two months in Jakarta, they should be recognized. The type and amount of recognition should vary with the magnitude of the accomplishment, but even small accomplishments should receive a "good job" from the boss.

Many companies have a formal employee recognition program. If not, start your own. Recognition does not have to be synonymous with cash. In fact, giving money as a reward can be risky, and some believe that it is a demotivator rather than a motivator. It is difficult to craft a bonus program that is perceived by all, or even the majority of employees, as being positive and fairly executed. Employees are often resentful if they do not receive a bonus, or if it is not the amount they were expecting when they do.

There are a wide range of nonmonetary alternatives that are less risky, less costly, and can be more effective in rewarding performance as well as building motivation:

- Dash off thank-you notes to people for working those long nights.
- Make certificates for special accomplishments that the employees can display at their desks.
- Give someone an extra day off after they've worked the weekend.
- Keep company trinkets like coffee mugs or key chains on hand for "spot" awards all year.
- Send flowers, balloons, or a plant to a spouse who, because of your project, hasn't seen his or her better half in the daylight for the last month.
- Give gift certificates for a dinner for two, so that the award recipient can share it with someone special.
- Give tickets to a baseball game or the theater.

Recognize people privately, but also recognize them publicly at staff meetings or awards ceremonies. It doesn't seem like recognition if no one knows about it. In one company I was with, we regularly surveyed the over 100,000 employees to find out what they viewed as most important in their jobs. They were given a list of 20 things to prioritize including salary, benefits, working conditions, and recognition. Year after year, recognition was number one. In one employment survey from another source, 26% of the people who left their companies did so because of lack of recognition. You cannot afford to lose good people for lack of recognizing their accomplishments. Even a small recognition budget can be used creatively and effectively.

> *We came to a point at my company where we had to cut the cost of employee benefits. My human resources director developed three alternatives for cuts that would meet our objectives. We presented the three alternatives — reducing vacation time, having employees contribute to health insurance costs, and eliminating the employee recognition program (primarily parties, certificates, bonuses, and savings bonds). I expected the employees to vote to eliminate the recognition program. However, the vast majority voted to have employees contribute to health insurance costs. The recognition program was perceived to be an important benefit even for those who rarely received rewards.*

Managers should give all employees the chance to reach their potential, but provide a "safety net" to protect them when they fail.

Another aspect important to managers of people is fairness and equitability. You may have certain employees who outperform others or whom you personally like more. However, it is your job as a manager to treat them all courteously and fairly and give them all developmental opportunities, visibility, and an opportunity to reach their full potential.

People learn by doing, so you must let your people do things they don't know how to do. This is painful for those of us who are perfectionists, but we must let our people learn. This means some of them will fail some of the time, but that is a risk that is inherent in managing people. Good bosses will let their people stretch and take risks, but will provide a managerial "safety net" so that when they do fail, they will not fail too badly, and their careers will not suffer from the fall.

Inconsistency and constant chaos degrades employee morale and cuts into productivity.

Employees need to know what to expect from their bosses, and what their bosses expect from them. Inconsistency in terms of direction, goals, or temperament keeps employees in turmoil and cuts down on productivity. Even if you are in a volatile environment where your boss' direction changes with the wind, try to buffer your people from this as much as possible and present a clear, consistent front to them. Stay calm in the midst of chaos, and you'll have a better chance of directing your people through trying times.

Sometimes during long periods of intense pressure such as downsizing or during an acquisition, nerves will fray, and tempers will flare. Women should be especially careful to avoid outbursts or the display of wide mood swings even in these trying times. People tend to label a woman who publicly emotes as "emotional," even if she is far less emotional than her male counterparts.

In a myriad of ways, some difficult to predict, your employees will strongly influence your success, both while they are on your staff and in the future. Being recognized as a fair leader who can make tough decisions with humanity, build strong teams, support individual development, and recognize performance is a tremendous credential. People who do this become known as people who can attract and keep the best resources even in difficult circumstances. Such leaders are quickly recognized by management and earmarked for important projects — the kinds of projects that have visibility and lead to executive positions.

Chapter Seven

Managing Across and Other Management Challenges

Change is usual.

-Peter Drucker

MANAGING ACROSS

In today's reengineered corporations, we often don't control the resources we need to get our jobs done.

Because many companies now have restructured into workgroups or process teams, we will see fewer and fewer stovepipe organizations in need of hierarchical managers at the top. Instead, we will need more managers who can manage groups of people that include individuals from organizations outside of their normal span of control. These managers will need to know:

- How to select strategic members of their process or work teams
- How to negotiate to get resources they do not normally control
- How to motivate the employees who do not report "hard lined" to them

Because, for the most part, we are dealing with knowledge workers, they are looking for leadership, inspiration, intellectual challenge, and recognition for their accomplishments. If managers can provide those things to people in their workgroups, they will be able to motivate them regardless of how direct their reporting structure is.

In most jobs I've had, there have been some required resources outside of my line operation. It may have been human resources, finance, or administration, but there was typically some function outside of my group that I needed in order to be effective in my own job. What I've found in every instance is that if I made my goals and objectives known to the supporting organizations, they were more than happy to jump in and help out — even when it meant nights and weekends and personal sacrifice — *if* I made it clear what I needed at the beginning and *if* I recognized their efforts at the end.

It is absolutely imperative that people from outside who are supporting your organization feel like they are a part of things. I always make it a point to invite the support personnel to staff meetings, recognition meetings, win parties, and any other function that recognizes that they are a part of the *team*, even if they are not a part of the organization. Often I will use part of my organization's recognition budget to recognize personnel in other organizations who have made extraordinary contributions toward meeting our goals. It is always worth it.

One executive from a large East Coast financial firm started what she called a "bridge club." It consisted of people at work who had information she needed, but who were not in her direct control. The word "bridge" was used to connote bringing together these members from dif-

*ferent functional groups. The "club" signified its volun-
tary nature and informal atmosphere. The woman who
started the organization said, "They know their contributions are valued, and they appreciate the chance to exchange information across functional boundaries in an
informal setting that's fun."*

When building cross-functional or cross-organizational teams, it
is essential that you accept only the best people available, and that
you understand the shortcomings of the team members. One woman,
because of a series of circumstances, found herself with less than the
"A Team" on her project.

*We were putting a team together for a project for one of
my clients. Everybody was really strapped for resources,
and the available pool was less senior than what I needed.
Because of this, I was forced to put some of the staff in
"stretch" assignments. Normally, on a cross-organizational team, I have some senior people and some junior
people, but this time, my team was predominantly junior,
with the exception of a new hire who had never had an
assignment like this before. The team began to experience
problems, missing internal deadlines and producing lower
quality work for internal review. Because having a top
quality product for our clients is paramount, I ended up
redoing much of the work myself at great personal sacrifice.*

*My biggest disappointment is that the team members did
not ask for help when they needed it; this fact became apparent only at the review cycle at my level. Looking back,
I realized that I was managing this very junior team much
as I would have managed a team with a richer mix of seniority. I assumed they would ask for help — they did not.
I assumed they understood the importance of the internal
review process and that the review dates were inviolate —*

they did not. What I learned from this is that when in doubt about the quality or capability of an individual, overmanage until you are sure that you can get the desired results from the person in question. Make sure you inspect things early-on in the process and establish checkpoints sooner than you normally would so that you have time to rework or correct.

Cultivating peer relationships is essential to your acceptance — and therefore your success — in the organization.

Just as managing up and down the chain-of-command is increasingly crucial to success, so is managing peer relationships. Peers can significantly help or hurt your career, depending on your relationship with them. They can include you in their information networks and tie you into the culture and politics of the organization — providing you with valuable information that allows you to prepare for upcoming events — and keep you from being surprised by new developments. Or they can exclude you from their networks, keep you "out of the loop," and make sure that you are always one step behind and perpetually embarrassed.

Women often have to work extra-hard to develop peer relationships, especially if they work in male-dominated environments. Remembering that most women are assumed "incompetent" until proven otherwise, many male peers may not immediately see your value to the organization, and, if you are the only woman, they may view you as a "token."

How do you overcome these initial biases and develop strong peer relationships?

* Get to know your peers.
* Spend time with them.

- Find out what their goals are and whether you are competing for the same next job.
- Find out what they need to be successful and help them when you can.
- Build trust with them.

Your peers and co-workers must know that when you tell them something, your word is good. They must believe that you will always be there for them and that you will never betray a confidence or speak poorly of them in their absence.

Additionally, and this is especially important if you are rewarded based on team goals, your peers must view you as an asset to the organization rather than a drag on it. Make sure they know what you do and how it contributes to the overall team's success. This may require a little internal selling or public relations on your part, but it will be of paramount importance if it is even remotely possible that you will one day head the group of which they are a part. I have seen many people get passed over in the selection to replace their bosses because higher-ups perceived that they did not have the support of their peers for that job and that putting them in the job would result in a mutiny.

Even when peer managers have little interaction with you or your organization, they can be important to your success. It is imperative to be perceived as an honest team player who can be counted on for fair treatment. Gaining this reputation comes from:

- Being clear about your objectives
- Being honest in your interactions
- Showing an understanding of your peers' problems
- Whenever possible, lending a hand

When important or difficult assignments are handed out, managers who have the respect and support of their peers get selected. Management can feel more comfortable that such managers will be able to get the job done even if it involves gaining cooperation and support of those outside their direct control.

RISK-TAKING

Women are not socialized to take risks, but you can't get very far playing it safe.

Many women, because of the way they've been socialized, tend to be risk-averse in the choices they make in their careers, as well as in their individual jobs. Women tend to stay in jobs longer than necessary and with companies longer than they should. Many women turn down exciting assignments for which they are eminently qualified because they are comfortable where they are and perceive a change as high risk.

Risk is inherent in business. Every new product, every new market, and every new company face both identified and unidentified risks every day. Companies need executives who are willing and able to take on these risks and manage through them. Women should not be afraid to assert themselves and take these risks but should offset them by recognizing and understanding them in advance and mitigating them as much as possible.

Risk mitigation can be accomplished in a number of ways:

- Anticipate the worst-case scenario and understand the possible impact to schedules, budgets, and staffing to ensure that you have adequate reserves of people and funds to bail you out, if need be.
- Prepare contingency plans for high-risk scenarios and ensure that those involved in implementing any contingencies are well-informed of the risks and the mitigation strategies.
- When you are engaged in a high-risk situation, make sure your manager is aware of the situation, as well as the contin-

gency plans, and will support you should the worst-case scenario actually happen.

Managers should always be aware of their company's tolerance for risk. What may be considered a perfectly acceptable calculated risk in one company is considered an unacceptable risk in another. Wall Street traders routinely put hundreds of millions of dollars at risk, but in most corporations, losses of even a few million are considered unacceptable. Do not find yourself in a position where you have made a grave error in judgment regarding what your corporate culture will accept. Also, do not back yourself into a corner so that you cannot get help from others in the company in the event of a catastrophic failure.

MANAGING CRISES AND CONFLICT

By handling crises and conflicts with preparation, sensitivity, and finesse, you can minimize the negative impact on the organization.

A business organization is a microcosm of life. The larger the organization, the more opportunity there will be to experience a sampling of the conflicts and crises that occur in "the real world." Types of situations I, or managers I know, have had to deal with include:

- Telling an employee a parent has died
- Telling an employee a spouse had died
- Having an employee die at the work site
- Dealing with employees sexually harassing other employees
- Dealing with one employee stalking another
- Telling employees that their co-worker was killed by her husband and was found in a barrel under her house
- Telling employees their co-worker has committed suicide

127

- Having an employee arrested and convicted of murder
- Having a male employee who had a sex change operation over vacation show up to work at the factory in a dress to make a point (standard attire was a company-furnished jumpsuit)
- Dealing with hostile employees who physically threaten you when you try to defend corporate policy

One woman tells how she feared for her safety during an event at work:

At one point in our company, we changed our policy on how to pay overtime to hourly workers. We used to pay them overtime for each hour beyond eight in a given day. They could actually work four 10-hour days, and get paid overtime for those two extra hours each day. We decided to change the policy to pay overtime only to those people who worked more than a standard 40-hour week. We had a substantial number of data entry clerks who were impacted by this, as they often worked long days right before the payroll went out. They were very upset with this change in policy and asked that I, the director in charge of the business unit where they worked, come out and address their concerns.

I did visit the site, and we looked hard for a room that would accommodate all the people. We ended up in an empty room with no furniture. The result was that the employees lined the walls, and I stood in the middle of the room like a target. They proceeded to verbally attack me and hurl insults at me and the company. I honestly feared for my safety. I think the only thing that saved me was that I was well-prepared, didn't back down, and showed them I understood the severity of the situation to them. If I had it to do over again, I would have controlled the environment better and had the room set up theater-style in advance.

When dealing with these types of crises or conflict situations, make sure that you:

- Are well-prepared to handle them. Practice what you will say, and role play with others if necessary. Know your position and don't back down.
- Display sensitivity to the employees.
- Know your emotional limitations and bring help (e.g., your manager or human resources representative) if needed.
- Know when to be firm, serious, or humorous as the situation dictates.
- Know the company's policies regarding the situation (bereavement policies, ethics policies, etc.)
- Know the employee's legal rights as well as the company's legal position.
- Control the setting, whether one-on-one or in a group, and select the right room with the right ergonomics to make your message easier to deliver and more effective.
- Don't go into high-conflict situations alone.

By handling crises and conflicts with preparation, sensitivity, and finesse, you can minimize the negative impact on the organization.

MANAGING CHANGE

Companies that don't change can't survive.

Our economy, our country, and our businesses are undergoing a period of unprecedented change. Successful companies will respond to this change by reengineering, expanding, contracting, and flexing in other ways to keep up with the rapidly changing environments in which they operate. Companies that do not change will not survive.

Information-hungry managers and workers, seeing their worlds change around them, are snapping up copies of books on changing and dealing with change, from James Champy and Michael Hammer's *Reengineering the Corporation*, to Tom Peters' *The Tom Peters Seminar: Crazy Times Call For Crazy Organizations*. It's become apparent to us all, both intellectually and viscerally, that in order for our companies and ourselves to compete in this age of global cutthroat competitiveness, we must rethink the way we do everything. Peter Drucker summed this up with his statement, "Every company must be willing to abandon everything." *Everything*.

©1995, Washington Post Writers Group. Reprinted with permission.

Some companies have embraced this concept wholeheartedly and have induced radical change, from getting rid of their middle management, to selling the furniture, to abolishing titles altogether. In his second book, *Reengineering Management*, James Champy writes, "Radical change is sometimes, in some ways, the easiest to accomplish. Making a clean break with the past sends a mobilizing jolt of energy through the company, but only when people are given some sense of control over what happens next." With change coming rapidly and unpredictably, it's often difficult, if not impossible, to ensure that people feel a sense of control.

This lack of a sense of control has taken its toll on workers, both in terms of productivity and morale. In a recent study by Coopers & Lybrand, low morale and high stress were reported in the surviving employees in two-thirds of the companies that had recently downsized. In another study, taken by The Wyatt Company in 1994, 44% of respondents said that recent company changes were having a negative impact on "work climate and morale," and 42% felt overworked.

How we adapt to change and manage ourselves, our people, and our businesses through turbulent seas will have a major impact on our personal success in the next decade.

Imagine how you might feel if you work at Lotus and are managing the group developing the next generation of office products. One morning, you wake up, pour your breakfast cereal, and open the newspaper to discover that IBM has initiated a hostile takeover of Lotus. What flashes through your mind? *Will we still develop this product line? Will it look the same? Will all my past work on it be wasted? Will I even have a job? What will I tell the people who work for me?*

With takeovers, mergers, foreign competitors appearing overnight, wild currency fluctuations, unlikely competitors partnering, and a host of other unpredictable events happening almost daily, change is more the norm than the exception. How we adapt to change and manage ourselves, our people, and our businesses through the turbulent seas will have a major impact on our personal success in the next decade.

For many of us, it's frightening, or at least disconcerting, to see positions for which we strived for years being abolished altogether, throwing cold water on our well-laid career plans. For others, our current jobs may be eliminated, leaving us to search for new positions, many of which may only now be being created. Only one thing is certain. We will all somehow be impacted by the changes — whether it's our own job that's impacted, those of our spouses or friends, or whether we will simply be the ones left behind to do more with less after our co-workers have departed. Whatever our situation, we will not remain untouched.

Learn to live with it. It's been said that the only people who welcome change are wet babies. Most of us experience some level of discomfort or anxiety associated with change, especially when we have a lot of it in a short period of time or feel that we have little control over the outcomes. Even good change causes some level of stress in most of us. Unfortunately, change is now usual, rather than unusual, so we must accept that things may not, and probably will not, be the same from day to day in our work assignments, our companies, and our markets. Those of us who are used to structure and closure will have to get used to living with uncertainty and constant change. People who are unable to adapt to change face this as a major derailer in their careers. People who adapt well and take advantage of the new rules and the new structure will have countless and rare opportunities. Fortunately for women, they as a group score high on dealing with ambiguity and change and are actually strong change facilitators. This is a good time for women to leverage that strength.

Try to be flexible and adaptable. Flexibility and adaptability will be key words for people anxious to succeed in today's dynamic corporations. Companies that cannot turn on a dime and respond to changing markets and customer needs will not survive, and companies intent on survival cannot tolerate employees, especially managers, who will not support change. Both James Champy and Michael Hammer in their follow-up books to *Reengineering the Corporation* claim that in the instances where reengineering has failed, it was because the managers involved failed to reinvent their own jobs and management styles — mostly because they were threatened by a loss of power and a fear of change.

Career opportunities will come when you are able to buy into the change and get with the program. If you attempt to block the change and maintain the status quo, you are putting your company and yourself at risk. Resourcefulness is an area in which women have scored high in management assessments. To the extent that they can translate this skill into ways to leverage change to their advantage, they will make great inroads in their corporations.

Because technology is changing so rapidly and corporate velocity is tantamount to corporate success, continuous education is the only way we can stay competitive in today's marketplace.

Think resume. In *The Tom Peters Seminar: Crazy Times Call for Crazy Organizations*, Peters suggests that all employees, at every level, examine their resumes quarterly to see if they are growing and changing enough to be able to update their resumes with new data. If not, then they need to take charge of their own development and growth and ensure that they are making the significant contributions and experiencing the significant learning that would be "resumeable." He goes so far as to suggest that managers should have quarterly "resume contests" to see which employee has the most improved resume over the period. Because technology is changing so rapidly and corporate velocity is tantamount to corporate success, continuous education is the only way we can stay competitive in today's marketplace. Don't let your skills get outdated and tomorrow's technology pass you by.

Make a job. Peters also suggests that corporations should allow employees to be sufficiently empowered to "make" their own jobs. This concept is especially important in companies that are being reengineered because no one has ever been in the new jobs before, and such positions are apt to be ill-defined. If you personally are in a newly created or ill-defined job, create your own role clarity. Don't wait for someone else to define all aspects of your job for you. If something needs to be done or a decision needs to be made, empower yourself — and just do it. If you are the manager of the employees with the "new" jobs, your goal should be to excite and motivate them enough to make them want to "make a job" and take charge of something because "someone needs to do it." "Job-making" is a valuable skill for employees and managers in companies in the midst of mammoth and perpetual change.

Communicate, communicate, communicate. Communication is always important in any organization, but in times of change or turmoil, it takes on an even greater role. (See more on communicating in Chapter Ten.) Many people always assume the worst in times of downsizing or restructuring. If you have to downsize or lay off, communicate the extent of the change upfront and make sure the individuals involved have as much warning as possible, to enable them every opportunity to find employment elsewhere. Make sure, also, that the employees who are not involved know who they are and are reassured that they are secure, or you run the risk of having them look outside and leave when you don't want them to go.

Even when companies are not downsizing but are in turmoil through restructuring or reengineering, communicating with employees to share everything possible is a must. Managers must gain the trust of their employees by sharing, rather than hiding, information in times of uncertainty. If we expect our employees to ride the wild bronco of change and stay in the saddle with us, we must arm them with enough information to allow them to feel a part of the action and have some control over the outcome.

MANAGER AS ROLE MODEL

The higher in the organization you rise, the more people pay attention to everything you say and do. Make sure your messages are what you want them to be.

As managers and leaders, everything we do is symbolic to our employees. How much time we spend on each agenda item in a meeting sets the tone for what's important to us. If we claim that customer satisfaction is our number one priority, but we never visit customers ourselves or never measure or discuss their satisfaction in our staff meetings, what credibility does that have with the staff?

If you say that quality is key in the organization, but have your quality control people reporting at the lowest levels and have no meetings or briefings on your calendar to keep you informed, it will be hard to convince others that you are sincere.

Are you having a cost-cutting binge and asking the employees to make sacrifices? You'd better not be caught taking a limo to the airport and flying first class, or you will lose the loyalty of the employees who are being asked to make the cuts.

What about the way you communicate? Is it professional? Is it consistent? Be aware that every note you scribble in every margin, every e-mail, and every voice mail should be a model for your employees and may be copied over and over by them and distributed to their peers. Make sure that you would never be ashamed or embarrassed if your messages, written or verbal, were mass distributed.

In other words, make sure that your behavior sends the signals that you want:

- Your messages, in every form, are clear, concise, and professional; and you would be proud to see them distributed.
- Your meeting agendas reflect your true priorities.
- Your calendar reflects your true priorities.

- Your behavior is consistent with the behavior you expect of your people.
- You follow your own policies and procedures.

People learn by modeling the behavior of others. Make sure you're teaching the right behavior.

Chapter Eight

Networking

Obscurity is not a virtue

-Peter Drucker

THE IMPORTANCE OF NETWORKING

Today networking is more important than ever. With fewer hierarchies and more cross-functional (and organizational) workgroups, getting things done through formal mechanisms and chains-of-command often just doesn't work.

Men have long recognized the importance of networking in getting their jobs done and progressing in their careers. The professional associations, men's clubs, the golf course, and even the local bar have long been venues men have used to build the relationships that help them work out problems, acquire assistance and resources, and find jobs.

When women entered management in large numbers in the 1970s, they were slow to build similar networks. In the tough, all-consuming struggle to gain acceptance and succeed, there was little time to develop the formal and informal forums that were already in place for men. Moreover, at the time, there was a feeling held by many that women weren't interested in networking with other women. Some female executives wanted to get into "the men's club" and perceived that women's networks lacked power and were ineffective. Also, it was believed that the women who had "made it on their own" didn't want to reach down and help other women.

That is not to imply that women were unfamiliar with networking. Women's networks had thrived in the community for a long time. Most women who stayed at home in traditional roles understood the value of the car pool, coffee klatch, the PTA, and the bridge club in getting things done and increasing their success in the community. Perhaps these tactics were discounted by young women in business in the 1970s as a result of their desire to strike out on their own and discard the experiences of their stay-at-home mothers. Perhaps other women viewed being associated with a woman's organization as "politically incorrect" when most were trying so desperately to blend in with their male counterparts. Whatever the reasons, strong women's networks were not common in business, and most women struggled alone to keep up with their male counterparts, who in turn were benefiting from deals and opportunities created in the men's club.

Today networking is paramount to success. In most jobs, we are measured on how effective we are at getting things done. With fewer hierarchies and more cross-functional (and organizational) workgroups, getting things done through formal mechanisms and chains-of-command often just doesn't work. The relationships we build within the company and throughout the business community have become essential. It is through these largely informal networks that we form the bonds and establish rapport with individuals who can help us gain the resources, support, and information we need to get things done. Also, in tight economies, with increasing demands for skill and performance, every new hire has become strategic. In companies that sell labor — such as law firms and consulting organizations — leaving jobs unfilled is tantamount to leaving money on the table. Using networks to identify quality resources reduces the time required to identify candidates, as well as the risks of hiring someone totally unknown.

USING NETWORKS

When looking for a job, a candidate to fill a job you have open, or looking for resources for a project or team, networking, if done correctly, will be more effective than any other means of search.

Networking for jobs and resources. Hiring people you know, or at least whom someone you trust knows, minimizes risk and ensures that you meet your hiring objectives. Many companies, including the high technology, knowledge-based companies, recognize this and have implemented employee referral programs that offer cash incentives to employees who recommend friends who are subsequently hired by the firm. Employee networking is substantially cheaper than advertising or using a search firm and usually produces a higher quality candidate.

At the higher levels, *most* jobs are filled through networking, internally as well as externally. Recall how Lou Gerstner, when taking over the troubled IBM, replaced most of his senior staff with people he knew and trusted. With IBM bleeding to death and the board of directors breathing down his neck, Gerstner could ill afford to take chances on a staff he neither knew nor trusted, regardless of their qualifications and competence. When looking for a candidate to fill a job you have open or looking for resources for a project or team, networking, if done correctly, will be more effective than any other means of search.

Likewise, if you are the candidate looking for a job, networking is your best alternative as well. Letting people in positions of power or influence know that you are looking for a job or are willing to consider a change results in a higher success ratio than sending out resumes or letters or, in most cases, even working with a recruiter.

> *I went to a women's conference sponsored by the senior women in my company. I wasn't sure what to expect, or even what I wanted to accomplish by attending. I decided just to go with an open mind and see what the conference was all about. First off, I was surprised by how many women had come from all over the country at their own expense — more than 600. Then, I was pleasantly surprised at how open and caring the women were toward each other — how much they wanted to help each other. I met several women in workshops and at meals with whom I exchanged cards. We did a pretty good job of keeping up with each other during the year and keeping each other informed about what was going on in different parts of the company. At the next year's conference, we saw each other again and renewed friendships. I also met several new women. Over time, I built up quite a network. We helped each other staff a number of key jobs. One year, I got a call from a woman I hadn't heard from in a while. There was an exciting job opening up in the division that she was in. She remembered my background and knew that it was a perfect match. She got me in the door to interview with her boss before anyone even knew that the job was coming open. He and I hit it off, and he agreed that the match was right. I ended up getting the job — a job I never would have even heard about except for the networking I had done.*

Many women find that it is exhausting for them to be forced to draw from their masculine sides all day — due primarily to our male-dominated business climate. John Gray describes how women can get re-energized just by having an opportunity to use their feminine sides and express themselves as women.

Networking for support. Women who work in a predominantly male environment need to network with other women sometimes just to share experiences and gain empathy and advice from other women regarding some of the unique challenges they face in the workplace.

There was a point in time when I was the only woman in my organization. My boss was a man, my peers were all male, and my direct reports were all men. I didn't realize how hungry I was for the opportunity to have some business contact with other women — a chance to express my feminine side sometimes at work — until I hired a female deputy. That simple act changed the entire dynamics of my organization and gave me a portion of my day when I could relate to someone else "woman-to-woman." I didn't realize how important this was until I was reading a passage in John Gray's book, What Your Mother Couldn't Tell You and Your Father Didn't Know, *in which he discusses how exhausting it is for women to be forced to draw from their masculine sides all day, due primarily to our male-dominated business climate. Gray describes how women can get re-energized just by having an opportunity, a few minutes at a time, to use their feminine sides and express themselves as women.*

Fortunately, with our current knowledge-based work force, women can now use more of their feminine sides in their everyday management. Coaching and facilitating skills that they once hid while working in rigid command-and-control hierarchies are now recognized as vital. Women's consensus and team-building skills are now encouraged in the new world of workgroups and teams. Hopefully, as the economy continues to shift, businesses will evolve to the point where women have a balance in the use of their feminine and masculine sides at the office.

Networking with others, inside and outside our companies, is key to staying tied into the human networks on which our most vital information travels.

Networking for information. In many instances in our careers, the speed with which we gain information and the accuracy of that information impacts how quickly and how well we make decisions. Networking with others, inside and outside our companies, is key in staying tied into the human networks on which our most vital information travels.

Good networkers get "heads up" information on impending organizational changes, new projects, or job assignments about to be opened up, and a host of other items that are high-impact from a career perspective. Being "in the loop" allows you the opportunity to influence decisions before they are announced, or at least to develop a strategy for dealing with changes before they are made public. Being "out of the loop" ensures that you are always in reaction mode and have less control over your career than you could have.

Networking can also directly help you get business, as one woman recalls:

> *Often, I give industry-specific speeches or talks. These talks are attended by many of our clients, as well as by people who are only prospective clients. I've found that if I stay afterwards and really network with the attendees, I will get a lot of information about their companies and their upcoming projects. This is especially critical in our industry, where much of our work comes from proposals.*

Often, the companies will request proposals and give you only a week or so to respond — nearly an impossibility considering the level of detail they require. I've found that by networking after my talks, these people will usually call me later and give me a "heads up" on when their requests for proposals are coming out. Sometimes, they'll even bounce ideas off me to see if they're reasonable to include in the request. This tiny bit of information — about timing as well as content — can translate into a huge advantage in the marketplace.

BUILDING NETWORKS

When looking outside the company, call on your outside business associates. If they cannot help personally, see if they can make introductions to others who may be able to assist you.

Working your contacts. Your best sources are the people you know both inside and outside of your company. If you are looking to make an internal move or fill an internal position, call key co-workers for ideas and recommendations. Who are the key people? They are the people who've built wide informal networks. They have a reputation for knowing where the jobs are and who the good employees are. A secondary benefit of going to such people often is that you will build an in-depth knowledge of resources and opportunities in the company. Over time, you will be the key resource for others when they need jobs or positions. Your power and influence in the organization will increase tremendously.

When looking outside the company, call on your outside business associates. Make them aware of your situation and solicit their advice or help. If they cannot help personally, see if they can make introductions to others who may be able to assist you. It is common for peers in other companies, even companies in competition with yours, to use each other in this manner. And just as with internal contacts, the more you do this, the wider and deeper your network will become and the more influential you will be perceived to be in the business community.

Building new contacts is easy, too — if you are always on the lookout.

> *I've made valuable business contacts at Christmas par-*
> *ties, cookouts, on airplanes, and on the golf course. Some*
> *of the best contacts I have made were at a business golf*
> *tournament where it rained. We all ran inside to the club*
> *house and sat there talking for two hours while we waited*
> *to see if the rain would stop. I actually met many more*
> *people than if we'd been able to finish our game. The con-*
> *tacts I made at that tournament allowed me to help some-*
> *one find a job and also helped me find a partner for a*
> *strategic alliance.*

Because I never know when opportunity might strike, I always tuck a few business cards in my purse or pocket, regardless of where I'm going. I'm never sorry.

Once you have the contacts in place, mark your calendar to call periodically on these people in order to keep your relationship current.

Use the occasion of company-sponsored events to build relationships with others who can include you in their information loops.

Building networks inside the company. How does one begin to build networks? Internally, building relationships with those in all parts of the company is critical. If your position doesn't provide opportunities to do this, volunteer for task forces, get involved in company training programs, have lunch in the company cafeteria on a regular basis, and attend company parties and all open meetings (such as division all-hands meetings). Use these occasions to have conversations with people from different departments or organizations. Compare notes. Find out what they know that you don't. Build relationships with others who can include you in their information loops. One woman tells what worked for her:

> *Becoming a volunteer management training facilitator shortly after joining a new company allowed me to meet peers, human resources representatives, and management candidates from all over the company. Since I was a facilitator, I was perceived to be an authority figure, which immediately increased my stature among the staff. As a result, my name is recognized throughout the company, and I know where to find resources when I need them. Other employees quickly forgot that I was the "new girl on the block" and began to treat me like one of the "good old boys" in the informal power structure. Most people believe that I've been with the firm for years longer than I have, and they look to me when they need people or advice.*

Use all opportunities to meet people in your business community. Keep in touch with people even when the contact is not obviously useful to you — and never burn bridges.

Networking with business associates. Clients, business associates (such as teammates on a project or people working for different companies but for the same client), and even competitors can become a part of your network. When building networks:

- Keep track of co-workers after they leave your firm.
- Get to know the managers from other firms with which you do business.

- Keep up with clients even after the job ends.
- Use the people you know to introduce you to others who can be helpful. Attend trade associations, meetings, conferences, or seminars where you are likely to meet others in your industry.
- Peruse the list of conference attendees, and target those who might be of help to you.
- Introduce yourself and exchange business cards with people you meet on airplanes, in seminars, on the golf course.

These are a few of the ways successful businesswomen build networks. The key is to use all opportunities to meet people in the business community. Keep in touch with people even when the contact is not obviously useful to you — and *never* burn bridges.

You'll find that interacting with other women is rewarding and fulfilling, but don't ignore men and their networks. Networking only with women limits the breadth, depth, and power of your personal network.

Using networking organizations. Today there are many networking organizations, and it has become much easier to get into one or several. Look for women's business networking organizations such as Women in Technology, Women in Telecommunications, National Association for Female Executives, or a host of others that specialize in helping businesswomen meet others who share their issues and are also interested in networking. Many large corporations now have internal women's networking groups, as well.

One Fortune 500 company has an incredibly successful organization for management women. It started as a small group of women meeting in the kitchen of one of the members and over a 10-year period blossomed into a major annual conference attracting more than 600 women world-

wide. The women use the conference for skill-building, experience-sharing, and networking. The conference has become so large and visible that the CEO of the corporation is often the keynote speaker. At least two job changes in my career — both promotions — were a result of networking with other women at this particular conference.

A group of senior women — Senior Executive Service (SES) — in one government agency started an internal networking organization. They met with the top executives of the agency to raise their awareness of women's issues at work. Agency top management views this group of women as very powerful, because of the raw talent contained in their ranks, as well as their focus and dedication to solving the issues of women in the agency. Interestingly enough, there are some SES-level women there who have declined to join the group because they don't want to call attention to themselves by being associated with a women's organization. They feel they are better off "blending in with the men." When you are outnumbered five-to-one, as the SES women are by the SES men, it is hard, however, to "blend in."

If your organization doesn't have a women's networking organization, consider starting one. It's important for women to help, mentor, and support other women — both intracompany and intercompany. I cannot overemphasize this. If women won't help other women, how can they expect men to help them?

While you'll find that interacting with other women is rewarding and fulfilling, don't ignore men and their networks. More and more, men are including the women they respect and trust in their circles. And, like it or not, men still hold many of the keys to success. Networking only with women limits the breadth, depth, and power of your personal network. Make sure in your dealings with men that you educate them on the importance of networking with women. Emphasize the positive aspects to them, the benefits they will derive by including a whole new circle of resources in their networks. Ask men to refer women they know to networks you are in, or refer you to networks they are in. Most men just don't think about including women. Help them think about it.

Be sure to understand the limitations of the networking medium you choose and make certain that it will meet your needs for privacy, confidentiality, and results.

Networking electronically. With the wide acceptance of the Internet, company e-mail, and services such as America Online, it is now possible for most people to network electronically. Electronic bulletin boards now advertise jobs, special interest organizations, and users' groups. Users can send and receive mail and get almost instantaneous responses. This can be a very positive tool, in that it can instantly expand your information, support, and job networks by connecting you to thousands of other users worldwide. It has its downside, however, that should be noted:

- **It's not very personal.** Most of the people with whom you will communicate will be strangers and will remain so.
- **It has no body language.** Communicating electronically strips all the nonverbal signals from our communication. This is especially troublesome for women, who typically use many of their senses to pick up a variety of nonverbal signals that help them interpret the other party's real message.
- **It's not very private.** Anything you post on a bulletin board can be read by thousands of others, some of whom you may prefer not see what you wrote. Intracompany e-mail belongs to the company and affords little or no privacy. Be certain that you don't send something to a bulletin board or out e-mail that you don't want widely distributed. A recent e-mail note between lovers at *The Washington Post* found its way into print in the next week's paper — complete with the first names of the participants.

Be sure to understand the limitations of the networking medium you choose, and make certain that it will meet your needs for privacy, confidentiality, and results. Networking is an important activity, and you want it to have positive results.

Chapter Nine

Fitting In — Culture, Image, and Politics

Always treat your image — indeed your whole career — as a product that you are managing and marketing.

-Paul Stern

FITTING INTO THE CORPORATE CULTURE

Understanding your company's corporate culture and being able to deal with it are essential to your happiness in your career.

My first job out of college was as a production engineer working for a Fortune 3 oil company. Part of my job was to manage a crew of laborers offshore in the Gulf of Mexico, on a platform that drilled for and produced natural gas. These men, yes, they were all men, worked two weeks straight and then had two weeks off. During their two weeks "on," they never left the platform. They ate, slept,

151

and worked all in the same place. Needless to say, this was a very "manly" place, never before invaded by a woman. They didn't exactly welcome me. In fact, you could describe their treatment of me as hazing — only it was much worse than what I imagine most fraternity pledges are subjected to.

I had to make a make-shift bed in the tool shed, because they had only one big room for all the men to sleep in, and I couldn't stay in there. The sheets they gave me to use were filthy. Much to my horror, the soap they gave me was covered in pubic hairs. I was going over some drawings with one of the men out on the platform, and in the middle of our meeting, he decided to relieve himself over the side of the platform — while I tried everything in my power to maintain eye contact. No matter what happened, I never reacted externally, and by the end of the first week, the harassment just stopped. I never told my boss or anyone else back in the office because I felt they were looking for an excuse to declare having women offshore a failure. By the end of the first year, we had set new records on the platform for production and safety.

Joining most new companies isn't usually this difficult, although there is generally a period in which new employees are tested to see how they fit in with the culture and the politics of the corporation. Since all companies have personalities and cultures, understanding them and being able to live with them are essential to your happiness in your career while there. Some companies are very formal and bureaucratic. Others are more collegial and relaxed. Some are leading-edge and promote risk-taking, while others are risk-averse and conservative.

A bad cultural fit is like a bad marriage — only counseling won't help. Sometimes, only divorce will fix the problem.

When interviewing for a job in a new company, ask lots of questions about the culture. Gain an understanding of the decision-making process, the level of empowerment of the employees, the amount of risk-taking that is tolerated, and what is considered "fast track". If you want to make vice president by the age of 35 and the youngest VP they've ever named is 50, the culture may not be a good fit. If feeling empowered is important to you, but the company you are considering requires 10 signatures for a capital acquisition, you might want to look around some more.

Remember, when you are interviewing, you are assessing them as well as being assessed. Most interviewers are impressed by candidates who come armed with questions about the company and culture because it shows an understanding of the importance of fitting in. One female recruiter gives this advice:

> *The interview process is truly a courtship between client and candidate. I encourage candidates to exercise as much scrutiny and analysis as they would when entering into any relationship that will consume more than half of their waking hours and one-third of their sleep. You spend more time — both consciously and unconsciously — on your career than people have traditionally spent on marriage or family relationships. This is unfortunate, but true, so "inspecting what you expect" is of the essence. Client companies will do thorough reference checks on you — both formally and informally. Do your own reference checks. Who had this position previously? Why did they leave? Were they fired? Promoted? If they left the company, use your own resources to determine why, and how they were treated upon resignation. If you learn how this organization treated others at divorce time, you'll know how they'll treat you during the marriage.*

Women who enter corporations near the top often find fitting in tougher than those who enter near the bottom. Because there are so few women at the upper levels, many women feel isolated and, in essence, are an anomaly in the executive suite. This creates tremendous stress on those women who must adapt to the previously all-male environments with no support and no empathy.

What makes this especially challenging for women is that the higher up one enters the corporation, the more important fitting in is. At the highest levels, you *represent* the company, internally as well as externally. Women at all levels, *especially* upper levels, need to help and support each other through the trying times of adapting to a new culture.

Many cultures put senior women "under a microscope" in their jobs. They are expected to represent "all women" to senior management, and they are expected to be role models to the women below them in the organizational structure. This constant inspection — from above and below — can be very stressful when it is added to an already full plate of demands from bosses, clients, employees, and peers.

On the other hand, some cultures have evolved to the point where they recognize the importance of women as managers, leaders, and spokespeople for their companies. Many of these companies provide opportunities to senior women to represent the companies in recruiting efforts and public speaking engagements. If there are few women at these levels, they are called on more often than their male counterparts to represent the company, and therefore get a healthy dose of visibility that they would not get in companies less conscious of women's strengths.

It is possible, even after asking all the right questions upfront and determining that the company is a good fit, to find that you have made a mistake and simply cannot fit in with the culture in a certain company. If this is true for you, make a move to a company that is better suited to your personality and temperament. Unless you are the CEO, you cannot change the culture of the company! Assess your resume and the number and frequency of your job changes to determine how soon you can safely make a move. If you have been a frequent job-hopper, you may want to stay for two to three years. If not, you can safely leave as soon as you determine the fit is not good.

If the cultural fit did not work out, and you begin to interview, be honest with the future employer. The former company may be wonderful at what they do, but you just didn't fit in with the organization. This doesn't make anyone bad or derelict in their job responsibilities; it just means that the comfort level wasn't there, and you think you would be happier and more productive elsewhere. If, however, you had a political falling-out with your former employer, be cautious about how you express the situation. Employers tend to be more attuned to the way other employers think, rather than the way employees think. They may not view the situation the way you do, so word your responses carefully.

CULTURAL CHALLENGES OF INTERNATIONAL BUSINESS

If you do not blend in with the culture of the country in which you are trying to do business, you will not be successful.

With today's multinational corporations, it is likely at some time that you will deal with cultures other than those of the U.S. Believe it or not, they can be even more trying than ours. One woman recalls just how trying:

> *I was working on a large telecommunications contract —*
> *one where many vendors wanted to vie for the few subcon-*
> *tractor positions available. One of the subcontractor*
> *wannabe companies was Japanese. They had scheduled a*
> *meeting with my boss and me to review what they could*
> *bring to the team. As I did with all the potential subcon-*
> *tractors, I prepared a presentation to explain what we were*
> *looking for, so that they could emphasize those points in*

their presentation. The representatives arrived from the Japanese company. They were all men — many of whom did not speak English. We went through the introductions, and as I prepared to start my presentation, the guests huddled and spoke rapidly to each other in Japanese. As the huddle broke up, the spokesman turned to my boss and said, "We would like the woman to leave." Shocked, he explained to our guests that the subcontractor decision was largely mine, and that if they wanted to be considered, they needed to make their presentation to me. The group huddled again and spoke to each other only in Japanese. Once again, the spokesman said, "We would like the woman to leave." My boss stood his ground, I stood my ground, and the meeting broke up. Even though they were in the U.S., they refused to adapt to our culture, and it cost them business.

While we may be dissatisfied with the progress women have made in U.S. corporations, the truth is women in the U.S. are light years ahead of their counterparts in most of Europe, Asia, or South America. A recent *Wall Street Journal* article compared the plight of working women worldwide:

- In Japan, many highly educated women are given only clerical jobs that they are expected to hold temporarily — until they get married and quit. They are considered "unhirable" if they are married. They are "unhirable" if they live alone. Small steps that Japanese women pursuing careers had made in the past few years have been reversed as the economy worsened and more men were out of jobs.
- In Sweden, where nearly 90% of the women work outside the home, only 17% of managerial-level positions are staffed by women, as opposed to 43% in the U.S. The country's liberal maternity policy — almost a year of paid leave — makes many companies hesitant to hire or invest in women.

- In Mexico, women are leaving corporations in droves to start their own businesses. The common corporate practice of requiring women to take a pregnancy test prior to employment, and then firing the women if they become pregnant later, has left women who want families few choices but to go out on their own.

When women work for multinational companies, foreign cultures often limit the opportunities those women have for international experience. While there are a few countries that will give women fairly equal opportunities — the U.K. for instance — this is not true everywhere, especially in parts of the Far East and Middle East. These factors must be considered when plotting career paths. While it's necessary for women to get experience in high-risk line jobs, it's foolish to target jobs where the culture will render you ineffective. Like the Japanese in the U.S., if you do not blend in with the culture of the country in which you are trying to do business, you will not be successful.

MEN'S DISCOMFORT WITH WOMEN IN BUSINESS

The current wave of political correctness has set women back. Men now have a heightened level of discomfort with women in the workplace, and most people simply do not want to entrust their careers and companies to others with whom they are not comfortable.

Because most of our businesses were founded and are still staffed at the top by men, the model for executive behavior is still "male-like." Historically, this has created a problem for women because they are expected to act enough like the men to make the men comfortable, but not enough like them to make them uncomfortable. In other words, women must be tough, but not masculine; assertive, but

157

not pushy; decisive, but not domineering; feminine, but not sexy. This is certainly a fine line to walk, but the fact of the matter is that in most major corporations, the decision makers who assign top jobs are still men, and *people — be they men or women — simply do not want to entrust their careers and their companies to people with whom they are not comfortable.*

What can women do? The same thing as men, actually — only more of it. They can work to fit in with the culture of the company and to establish a level of comfort in their working relationships with their peers, bosses, and subordinates. The main difference for women is that it is harder in most cases to establish these comfortable relationships because most men have not had a tremendous amount of experience with, or exposure to, having women as friends, mentors, and confidants.

Women must establish these relationships and build the trust and comfort with their co-workers that they see among the members of the previously all-male "club." This starts by being themselves and being honest, trustworthy, and competent. The current wave of political correctness has actually set women back in this regard, because many men now have a heightened level of discomfort in the workplace and feel they must walk on eggshells around women and minorities. It is proper for all of us to have boundaries that we expect others to respect in terms of language, humor, and other behavior; but women must not get so carried away with this that no one can be comfortable working with them. One woman summed this up:

> *I have found it amazing when women can stand around the coffee machine and joke and use profanity and then become incensed and offended when men speak that way in front of them. I think all of this has far more to do with good manners rather than political correctness or sexual harassment. If we set standards that reflect good manners and politeness, we would need far less focus on lawyers or harassment suits. If we focus on productivity and mission-critical results while behaving politely, the respect of*

our colleagues — both male and female — will follow.
We aren't owed respect until we earn it.

When men have an underlying discomfort with women, it prevents women from gaining many networking and mentoring opportunities that are available to people with whom the men *are* comfortable.

One male friend of mine, who is a partner in a "Big Six" accounting firm, always takes a female staff member along when he is dining with a female recruit. This man is as open and unbiased as any man I know, but the current wave of political correctness and many cries of sexual harassment have made him uncomfortable entertaining a female recruit alone. Another senior partner in the same firm routinely has dinner with his male subordinates but considers it "too risky" to invite his female subordinates out alone. He fears that an innocent word or act could be misinterpreted, and he could end up being sued.

The fear that many of these men have is very real, and is exacerbated by media hype. The Clarence Thomas/Anita Hill hearings, as well as the hearings regarding the charges against Senator Packwood, have had a chilling effect on many men — especially because it has become apparent that it is often difficult to distinguish between actual harassment and merely annoying behavior. With fuzzy laws and unclear definitions, many men would rather steer clear of women altogether than risk doing something "inappropriate."

This underlying discomfort has set women back substantially, as it prevents them from gaining many networking and mentoring opportunities that are available to people with whom the men *are* comfortable. When men hesitate to mentor or socialize with women at work, the women should not take it personally — instead, they should examine if there is something that they can do to make the men more comfortable with them. Sometimes, just getting the subject on the table and discussing it openly is sufficient to break the ice. If we all tiptoe around the subject and act like it isn't an issue, it will never get fixed.

It is incumbent upon women to establish relationships of trust and comfort with their male co-workers and to set clear standards — that never waver — of what they consider acceptable treatment. Most men's discomfort centers around the lack of clarity regarding what is acceptable and what is not. The clearer women are, the more comfortable men will be. The man who won't honor clear standards and boundaries is a rare exception.

There is another level of discomfort some men have — the perception of "reverse discrimination." Many white males believe that with EEO programs and affirmative action, they cannot get a fair shake in the workplace.

> *I worked in an organization where we had a lot of "special interest" roundtables — for women, minorities, and any other group that wanted one. These forums gave the employees an opportunity to speak directly to top management about issues of concern. In one employee satisfaction survey, I had a number of white males make write-in comments about reverse discrimination. I decided to hold an unprecedented "white male roundtable."*

> *About a dozen men showed up. They seemed embarrassed to be in a roundtable and seemed uncertain what to say or do. I put up the same agenda I used in all the other roundtables. It reviewed demographics in our area and compared the statistics in our company and our organization to the demographics to see how well we were doing. Then we had an open session to discuss specific issues. The men were surprised to see that white men were 36% of the population and 43% of the work force, but they held more than half of the jobs in our company, and more than 85% of the management positions.*

Since they had felt that women and minorities were getting the bulk of the promotions, they were surprised to see that more than a quarter of the white males in our organization had been promoted in the past year. They were even more surprised to see that of the very top jobs in the company, the white male population exceeded 95%. When we got to the open session and I went to the flip chart to write down their issues, I found that they had none, except their perception that women and minorities were "taking all the jobs." I explored this perception with them. By the end of the meeting, they were less inclined to believe that there was a problem or that they were in need of a "special interest" group to represent their issues.

Many white males are not aware at all of the statistics in their organizations and how they compare to demographics. They have no sense of awareness that they are 36% of the population and 43% of the work force, yet they hold more than 95% of the top jobs in most of our organizations. The sense of entitlement with which most men have been raised clouds their perception of who is and who isn't "getting a fair shake."

IMAGE — THE NARROW BAND OF ACCEPTABILITY FOR WOMEN

Women are "marked" by the choices they make in their hairstyles, their clothes, their makeup, and even their titles.

One woman recalls how she changed her mind about what she believed was acceptable to wear to work:

When I first started selling, I wore red and orange dresses because I wanted to stand out when I went to my clients' offices. I didn't want to look like one of their employees. I think it got their attention when we first met, but when it came to making them feel comfortable, they definitely felt better when I blended in with their environment, looked like one of them, and understood their needs.

There is definitely a narrow band of acceptability in how women can look at work — not too masculine, not too feminine, well-groomed, and confident — never flashy, never overtly sexy, never sloppy. While there definitely are narrow guidelines for men in their dress as well (they wouldn't come to the office without a suit and tie, for instance), most corporate cultures seem to be more forgiving of men's total appearance.

One senior executive with whom I discussed this issue supported this observation as he recalled how he had counseled a woman subordinate on her appearance:

I knew I was about to be promoted and I really wanted this particular woman on my staff to replace me. She had the skills and was very deserving of the promotion, but I was very concerned about her appearance. She was overweight and her clothes were sloppy. She just didn't have the look of a senior executive in our company, so I counseled her, and she changed her appearance. Subsequently, she got the job, but I have to be honest with you; I'm not sure I would have had the same conversation with a man.

It is essential that a woman's dress, manner of speaking, and choice of being addressed cultivate an image that portrays competence and confidence and that fits in well with the company's culture.

Deborah Tannen, in her book *Talking 9 to 5*, makes the interesting observation that women are "marked" by the choices they make in their hairstyles, clothes, makeup, and even in their titles. She states that, "Whatever she wears, whatever she calls herself, however she talks," will be used to make assumptions about a woman's character and competence. "In a setting where most of the players are men, there is no unmarked woman."

Dr. Tannen is correct. I reflected on years of offsite management meetings where the players were told to come "business casual." For a man, there is no question what this means. Come in khakis and a sport shirt with slip-on casual shoes. For a woman, there are choices to make. Does she wear a dress? A skirt? How long should the hemline be? Does she wear slacks? A blouse? Should she wear a blazer over her blouse? Does she wear flats or heels? Can the shoes have open toes? What may seem like inconsequential decisions are very significant when a woman realizes that all of these choices come together to form an image that portrays to others how confident she is and how seriously she takes her career.

One recruiter tells this humorous story about image:

> I recruited an incredibly talented, experienced, and successful West Coast marketing executive for a Midwestern Fortune 500 corporation. My client phone-interviewed the candidate and was extremely impressed with her. He suggested that I not fly to Los Angeles to meet her, since he was planning a trip there and could arrange to meet her immediately. After their meeting, the client phoned me and said we were right, she is competent and experienced. However, did I realize that anyone with a mid-thigh leather skirt, stiletto heels, patterned hose, and severe makeup just won't make it in their Midwestern culture? As I struggled to maintain my composure on the phone, I couldn't do anything but agree. Who was to know? As much as you can't take the country out of the guy, I guess you can't take the city out of the gal!

It is essential that women's dress, manner of speaking, and choice of being addressed cultivate an image that portrays competence and confidence and that fits in well with your company's culture. Be attuned also to how conservative the images are in your company and behave correspondingly. Observe how the senior women in your company dress. If there are no senior women, or if you do not feel they are role models, observe the men. If the men all wear dark suits and white shirts with conservative ties, dress conservatively. If the men dress with more flair, you, too, can be more expressive.

It is not necessary to mimic the men's attire — like some women tried to do 20 years ago — but on the continuum from high-fashion to ultra-conservative, use the mainstream of your company as your guide. When in doubt, err on the conservative side.

One woman commented to me that she used to worry about her image only when she was with her clients, but she's found that her dress, language, and mannerisms count for just as much, if not more, in her company's internal politics. She also found that when she thought she was "letting her hair down" among friends or colleagues at work and confiding normal fears and anxieties about a challenging client or project, the men in her company thought she was "weak or stupid." She lets her hair down now only when she's away from work.

Many women allow themselves to be treated with less respect than would be afforded a man in the same position.

It is important that women assume the trappings and demand the respect commensurate with their positions, such as title and perks. Many women allow themselves to be treated with less respect than would be afforded a man in the same position, probably because men have traditionally held women in our society in lower esteem than women have held men. How women allow others to speak to them is as much a part of their image as how they speak themselves. If the men at your level are all addressed as "Mr." or "Dr.," rather than by their first names, you should be addressed by a formal title as well. For those women who do not have their doctorates, the choice of Ms. versus Miss versus Mrs. also marks them and opens them up to others' assumptions that they are either conservative and traditional or liberated and rebellious.

It is interesting to note how many times women call their doctors "Dr. Smith" while the doctors call the women "Mary." It's especially interesting when you realize that "Mary" is "Dr. Smith's" client, not the other way around.

This lack of respect follows women outside the office, too. Many women who travel extensively complain that they do not receive the same level of service on the airlines as their male counterparts, especially in first class. Flight attendants will reach across women to serve the men sitting next to them, all the while acting as if the women are invisible. One airline honors their top flier each year with a lunch with the CEO and a position on a roundtable that discusses that airline's service. Last year, the top flier was a woman. After getting over his initial shock that the honoree was female, the CEO asked her how his airline treated women. She gave him an earful. He seems to have listened, because women who fly that airline frequently say the service has gotten somewhat better. As women are recognized as more powerful consumers and demand the respect that accompanies their positions and purchasing power, the service they receive will improve.

It is not appropriate for you to push for perks that do not normally accompany your level or grade, but it is also not appropriate for you to be denied the perks or benefits common to your peers.

The area of perks is another one where women often come up short. Take note of the perks others at your level have. Does everyone else have a window office while you are stuffed into an interior closet? Don't tell yourself it doesn't matter. It does, in terms of creating the image that you are equal to your peers and carry the same influence and have the same clout they do. Do they all have wooden furniture and you have metal? Do they take limos to the airport and you take cabs?

It is not appropriate for you to push for perks that do not normally accompany your level or grade, but it is also not appropriate for you to be denied the perks or benefits common to your peers. In one company, a woman there found out, quite by accident, that the men's cellular phone accounts were being handled quite differently than the women's accounts. The company was paying for the men's entire bills, minus their personal calls. For the women, the company was paying only for their itemized business calls. The difference was the monthly fees and taxes, which, over time, amounted to quite a bit. Her "accidental" discovery of this discrepancy resulted in a published policy that treated everyone's cellular bills the same.

During any compensation negotiations, be specific about what you believe is commensurate in the industry with your experience and position level. Most perks and benefits are negotiable — be they club memberships, car, vacation, or family leave. A prospective employer may ask if you are currently enjoying these perks. If the answer is no, but you know that other companies with which you are interviewing offer them, you might mention that they are part of your prospective offers.

OFFICE POLITICS

As you move up the ladder, politics take on a more important role, and by the time you are in the executive ranks, politics heavily outweigh job performance as a success factor.

Politics, as defined here, are how you interface with others, with whom you interface, and the image you portray when you do. It involves knowing who makes decisions, their preferences, their hot buttons, and their sacred cows. It is not stepping on others on the way to the top, playing mind games, "brown-nosing," or gossiping.

Politics are a very real part of the way we do business in the world and simply cannot be ignored. Depending on where you are on the corporate ladder, politics can be a small or a large part of your job. There is a continuum of what percentage of your job is made up of politics versus job performance. For instance, in an entry-level technical or factory job, how you are viewed and promoted will be based almost entirely on job performance. As you move up the ladder, politics takes on a more important role, and by the time you are in the executive ranks, politics heavily outweigh job performance as a success factor.

If you doubt my point about politics versus performance at the upper levels, you need only pick up a business magazine or newspaper and examine executive compensation versus company performance. Many CEOs have been made rich by the very companies they ran into the ground. Roger Smith of General Motors nearly wrecked the company — an event Tom Peters calls a "near death experience" — before his board finally removed him. But he retired a rich man with a huge lump sum payment combined with a substantial pension. Even more astounding, the GM board recently voted to raise his already large pension.

By understanding the politics in your company, you will know how to spend your time and energy. You will know better than to suggest a project that will surely fail, or to kill a program that is the boss' pet project. You will understand who works well together and who does not, so that when building teams, you can make them more effective. Being a good politician shows that you understand the culture and are adept at getting things done inside it.

Sharon Pratt Kelly, former one-term mayor of the District of Columbia, admitted after her re-election defeat that the reason she lost was that she never learned to be a good politician. She had come to the mayor's job as a high-level executive from industry. No one ever doubted that she had the brains or the technical skills to do the job. The politics were her undoing.

Politics are almost as exciting as war, and quite as dangerous. In war you can only be killed once, but in politics, many times.

-Sir Winston Churchill

I can't leave this topic without addressing some other definitions of politics, although they are not my own. Many people believe that office politics include insidious behavior such as deception and stepping on others to get to the top. While this behavior is not encouraged, and is often tolerated in men, *it is almost always a derailer for women.* In her book *Breaking the Glass Ceiling*, Ann Morrison quotes one senior executive regarding the dangers of politicking, "The corporate structure can tolerate men who are overly political, but we don't forgive women for this. It's a killer."

Once again, it's a fine line for women. It's almost impossible to gain a senior position without knowing how to navigate through your company's political waters, but being "overly political" is deadly. Let intuition and acute observation be your guide to what constitutes "good" politics versus "bad" politics in your company.

Chapter Ten

Communicating

*Precision of communication is important, more
important than ever, in our era of hair-trigger
balances, when a false or misunderstood word may
create as much disaster as a sudden thoughtless act.*

-James Thurber

THE IMPORTANCE OF COMMUNICATING WELL

**How well we communicate in every medium will determine if we
are perceived as confident and in charge of our businesses, or
uncertain and tentative.**

Few things will affect a person's career as much as the ability to
communicate effectively. Our communication skills get us interviews
for jobs, obtain job offers for us, determine what assignments we
receive, what credit we get for our work, and what raises we get. We
use these same skills to sell our ideas for projects or process im-

provements to our companies, to sell our products and services to our clients, and to sell our ideas and authority to our employees.

In most jobs, we use a variety of types of communication, from one-on-one conversation, to presentations to large groups, to proposals, memos, letters, and white papers. How we come across in each of these methods of communicating will determine if we are perceived as confident and in charge of our businesses, or uncertain and tentative. Because people are so different, and different people like to receive information in different ways, communications professionals cite a "Rule of Seven," that states that important messages should be communicated seven different times, in seven different ways, to ensure receipt of the message.

Gender or personal style differences can cause conflict or confusion in communicating. Knowing the style of the person with whom you are communicating will allow you to tailor your style.

Otto Kroeger and Janet M. Thuesen wrote *Type Talk at Work*, a discussion of the Myers-Briggs personality types, that can help pinpoint communication preferences as well as interaction styles. It includes the 16 possible combinations of eight personality characteristics: introvert, extrovert, sensing, intuitive, thinking, feeling, perceiving, and judging. Your particular personality type is determined by answering a questionnaire about your personal preferences and attitudes and mapping your answers to the predefined personality categories. The book then expands on each of these categories and gives information on how the different personality types interact with each other.

This is of interest primarily because, from this exercise, you can determine how others prefer to communicate and interact in the work environment (informally versus formally, for instance) and how they prefer to receive data (succinctly versus with a long preamble). By knowing this, your communications with others possessing a style or preference unlike your own can go much more smoothly, and style conflicts can be minimized.

Because of the importance of crisp and accurate communications, many companies offer periodic team-building sessions in which they conduct exercises such as Myers-Briggs to facilitate better communications among team members. There are other methodologies, as well, although Myers-Briggs is the most common. It is not unusual to hear students of Myers-Briggs refer to themselves as an "ENTJ" or "INFP," referring to their personality mapping. Knowing your style preferences and how they complement or conflict with others is a giant step toward conflict-free communications. Additionally, most students of Myers-Briggs are able to appreciate that there are a variety of styles and interaction preferences and that one is no better than the other. They simply differ.

One-on-one conversation. During the course of our day, most of us will engage in a number of one-on-one conversations with our employees, bosses, peers, clients, and suppliers. We will use these interactions to negotiate for assignments, sales, resources, and any number of other things that will impact our futures. Women excel in this more intimate communication because it takes advantage of their interactive brains and ability to read people as they communicate. Pitfalls here for women center around gender style differences and personal style differences that cause confusion or misinterpretation. An aid here for any communicator, male or female, is to understand the style of the person with whom you are communicating and tailor your own style to be consistent, or at least not in conflict with the other persons.

Meetings. Most businesses have a tremendous number of meetings, where the parties in attendance attempt to resolve issues, work problems, or gain consensus on some item of importance. While women have historically been good facilitators and consensus builders, many women may not fare as well in meetings because of meeting behaviors in their particular organizations.

Women are often frustrated when men interrupt them in meetings or ignore their suggestions until they are repeated by a man.

Some women complain that men interrupt them in meetings and don't allow them to complete a thought. Others complain that they are able to complete their thoughts but are ignored — and later their ideas are reintroduced by a man who gets the credit for them. I've personally experienced both of these phenomena and have tried different strategies to counter them. First of all, I've tried to sit back and observe the meeting behavior in my particular organization.

It is true that men tend to interrupt women. But they also interrupt men. I noticed no difference in the number of interruptions of men or women by the men in the organization or the way they go about it. While initially frustrated by the interruptions and often feeling unable to get a word in edgewise, I have found ways to hold the floor while I am speaking, as well as to interrupt, in my own way, with my own style, in order to get my turn. When interrupted, use your own style to interrupt the interrupter, and gently but firmly say something like, "Excuse me, you must not realize I still have the floor." Or: "Bob, we're all anxious to hear what your point is, as soon as I finish mine." To get your turn, say something like, "When you're finished, I would like to make a point." Develop your own style. Be firm but polite.

I decided the most prudent path is to modify my style to fit in better with the culture. It's important to note that you should not adopt a style that is not natural to you; however, you can make modifications to your own style.

One thing that happened so often in one company that I thought it would nearly drive me crazy was the amount of posturing that went on in meetings. Things that my peers and I would agree on long before the meeting suddenly were not in agreement anymore, once the boss was in the room. Peers who had supported a project of mine outside the meeting suddenly were questioning why I would want to do such a thing — once they had an audience. After doing much reading and thinking about this subject, I came up with a technique that works. I call it the "when" technique. Rather than get in a snit with the person in the meeting, I ask them a "when" question. Like, "When did you decide to stop supporting this project that we planned together, Bill?" or "When did you change your mind about this issue? We were in consensus last time we met." The "when" question lets others in the room know that you did your homework — but your peer is taking advantage of the meeting situation to posture for position.

I have tried to change the meeting behavior in different organizations, but usually the culture was much stronger than I. I finally decided the most prudent path was to modify my style to fit in better with the culture. It's important to note that you should not adopt a style that is not natural to you; however, you can make modifications to your own style to make interactions more successful. Another important note is that throughout history, people have survived by adapting to the dominant culture. While people can be change agents — and women are especially good at this — cultures will not change overnight. Adaptation is tantamount to survival in the short-term.

Presentations. Good presentation skills are critical to any career because so much of your visibility will be through this communication medium. Many senior executives see people who do not report directly to them only during briefings or formal presentations. Unfortunately, the impression that is made during these brief encounters can have a significant impact on how you are viewed long after the briefing is over.

Most of your exposure to senior management will be in presentations. Be prepared. Practice, practice, practice.

Because much of what is evaluated by senior management is how confident you seem and how convincing you are, it is imperative to practice presentations many times before you have to give them, especially if they are to senior executives you don't often see.

- Ask your boss or someone else whose opinion you trust to dry-run the presentation with you.
- Practice in front of a mirror.
- Videotape the presentation, if possible.
- Try to anticipate questions you might be asked.
- Talk to others who have made presentations to the same executives to see how they react and what they like in terms of style, visuals, and timing.
- *Be prepared.*
- Make sure your visuals and supporting materials are flawless and top quality.

Because of the way we are socialized, most women prefer more intimate communication, but being able to speak effectively in front of a group is essential for people striving for top jobs. Some women who did not feel that they were strong public speakers have benefited from speech classes, drama classes, or speaking groups like Toastmasters. Many companies, recognizing the importance of communicating ideas to a group, provide presentations skill training to their employees. Whatever it takes, you need to be able to present ideas confidently and convincingly. Take charge of building your own skills through every means available.

Written communication. With people as busy as they are these days and with businesses as far-flung and global as they have become — you can't help but communicate in writing. Whether it's in memos, letters, proposals, or e-mail, at some time you will be judged on your writing skills. Most people in business have learned to write simply and clearly and to state their point with a minimum of words. If you are not one of them, there are a variety of business writing courses available to teach you.

One person who used to work for me wrote adequate letters, but getting them completed took an inordinate amount of pain and suffering. At my urging, he took a business writing course to learn how to organize his thoughts and put them down on paper *faster and easier.* With all the electronic helpers today — spell checkers, grammar checkers, dictionaries, and other tools — there is no excuse for written communications to be anything but flawless. Remember, they are a statement of what you consider acceptable quality — they spell out your standards for all the world to see. Let them see only your best.

Direction and goals should be so clear and consistent that you can laminate them on a business-card-size piece of paper.

Giving direction. Employees need to know what to expect from their bosses, and what their bosses expect from them. Inconsistency in terms of direction, goals, or temperament keeps employees in turmoil and cuts down on productivity. Direction and goals should be so clear and consistent that you can laminate them on a business-card-size piece of paper. Companies that have ever-changing strategies have low employee morale, high turnover, and lost productivity. One of the reasons many of President Clinton's staff members cited for leaving the administration prematurely was frustration with constantly shifting policy. At last count, Clinton had five different policies on Haiti. Which one does his staff implement?

Contrast this with the clear, consistent direction and leadership provided by President Roosevelt after the Great Depression and during World War II. He was able to rally an entire nation and rescue it from the jaws of the Depression. Later, he was able to move the entire nation as one force in the war effort.

CONFUSING SIGNALS

Men's and women's communication styles are different. This presents a real danger of women being misunderstood in a male-dominated workplace.

Knowing the importance of clear communication as it relates to your career, imagine, then, the danger, if you are a woman, of men being the predominant evaluators of your communications. Many best-selling books have been written on differences between men's and women's communication styles and the numerous misunderstandings that can result from these differences.

Authors such as Deborah Tannen and John Gray have taken care not to draw conclusions about which style is more appropriate or preferred, but the reality of the situation is that most senior executives, and therefore most of the decision-makers regarding top positions, are men. This is important for women to keep in mind, because some of the signals they send in their communications are confusing to men. Some of the most common are:

- **Being indirect.** Both men and women are indirect, but at different times and in different ways. Men are typically indirect when it comes to feelings and topics with which they are not comfortable. They are, however, extremely comfortable with power and control and tend to be direct when giving direction or asking others to do something. This explains in part why men are confused by women's indirectness in giving orders or asking for support.

Often, when women give direction to subordinates, they will soften the order by being indirect or overly polite. From the woman's point of view, their position has already put them in the "one-up" position, so they can afford to be indirect or excessively polite — their message is still clear, and their direction will still be followed by virtue of their position. Where this breaks down is if women are so indirect that the men who work with them or for them honestly don't know what they want. Another concern is that men may interpret this indirectness as weakness or indecisiveness. I have personally found that I must adapt my style to my audience. I am less direct with women and more direct with men. Since we all deal with multitudes of people with varying styles, flexibility in our own styles is key.

- **Being excessively polite.** Women tend to spend a great deal of time considering how their words and actions impact others. Most female bosses are careful not to embarrass or make their subordinates uncomfortable — more careful, even, than they are with their bosses. Women's business language is sprinkled with pleasantries such as "please" and "thank you" in an attempt not to offend. Women also smile more at work than their male counterparts. While all of this is part of women's attempt to make others more comfortable and to "connect," some men view this, again, as women's reluctance to take charge and assert themselves. Be cognizant of this and watch your audience. Take charge and be firm, when necessary.

- **Letting others save face.** Because most women believe that real power is in empowering others — a skill essential in managing knowledge workers — women do not typically join in the game of "one-up" where you are always trying to gain the upper hand at someone else's expense. Women will often let others save face, even if it puts the woman in the "one-down" position. For men who have grown up with the game of one-up, this must be puzzling indeed. Again, the danger here is that men may misinterpret women's willingness to be one-down in order to "connect" as a lack of strength or willingness to take charge.

- **Asking lots of questions.** For women who have been raised to be polite and show interest in others, asking questions is one more way to connect. Additionally, most women have been socialized to believe that it is acceptable to ask for help. As a result, many women ask what, if compared to most men, seems like a lot of questions in business. While we think we are connecting or clarifying, some men take this to mean that women know less about the subject matter than their male counterparts or that they are less competent. Women need to be conscious of this perception and choose carefully between getting real data that they need and appearing as confident and informed as their male counterparts.
- **Talking about problems.** When faced with a problem to solve, most men will act first, talk later. Most women will talk first, act later.

Intuitively, I'd always known this is true, but I never worried about it until I was reading John Gray's book, Men are from Mars, Women are from Venus. *Gray describes that men think that when women discuss problems with them, it is because women want men to solve their problems. As I read this, it occurred to me that if John Gray is right, my boss must think that I can't solve many of my own problems, and take an inordinate number of them to him to solve. Alarmed by this, and having prided myself on my problem solving skills throughout my career, I determined to test Mr. Gray's theory. When I discussed what I had read with my boss the next day, he confirmed that Dr. Gray was right. I explained to my boss that I thought I was merely keeping him "in the loop" while I solved the problem. We decided that the direct approach was best.*

From then on, I prefaced my conversations with him with, "I'm not asking for help, I'm just keeping you informed," or, "I really would like some advice with this one." In this case, being direct was necessary and far better than being misunderstood.

Be certain that when you are discussing a problem with a man, you are clear on whether you are seeking his help, otherwise, he will assume you are.

- **Not knowing when to stop talking.** Women talk more than men. We just do. In a typical day, women will use thousands more words than men. John Gray says it, Deborah Tannen says it, research supports it. This has the impact on many men of feeling that women are "too much talk, too little action." Women should be cognizant of this and ensure that they are not losing their male audiences by beating an issue into the ground or talking so much that they are perceived as "rambling."

While women are well-served by their "people" focus when communicating, to be most successful, women should concentrate on:

- Being more assertive and firm
- Eliminating rambling and disclaimers from their speech
- Being brief
- Being direct

DELIVERING NEWS

When you are delivering news down the chain, it is important that you own the message.

When you are the boss, one of your responsibilities will be to deliver news from higher up the chain down your chain-of-command. Knowing how to represent the company's desires and direction as if they were your own will be key to your success. Many managers, especially young and inexperienced ones, don't understand the importance of representing the "company line."

> *I had a young manager reporting to me who was very good technically and had good interpersonal skills, but could never muster the managerial courage required to present unpopular direction as his own. He presented everything as "they" are making "us" do something "we" don't want to do. He took sides, and he was always on the side of the employee. He pitted management against the employees in every communication with his "us" and "them" language. By presenting news in a negative light, it was nearly impossible to sell the ideas down the chain, and he was demotivating his people rather than motivating them. I worked with him extensively until he was finally able to understand that, as a manager of people, it was his job to take the company's direction and present it in such a way that it made sense to his employees and they could get on board with it, even if they might not like it. As he learned to present news in the most positive light, he found that his own support and enthusiasm were contagious, and that it became much easier to rally his troops behind the cause.*

In addition to delivering news down the chain, successful managers will need to deliver news up the chain. Employee issues, concerns, and need for help must all be effectively communicated upward. The idea here is to sell the employee issue and the appropriate solution up the line, while maintaining objectivity and fairness.

Communicating is like the old quote, "You can never be too rich or too thin." You can never over-communicate.

As a manager of people, how and how often you communicate will be a major contributor to your success or failure. I have come to believe that you cannot communicate too much or too often. I am amused by companies that spend long hours and large sums of money on strategic plans that they then mark proprietary, lock up, and fail to share with their employees. Who do they think will implement these plans if the employees don't know what they are? Likewise for operating plans. I am continually shocked when I discover that the employees who deliver the plans in many companies don't know what the plans and goals are. It's as if the companies tell them "work as hard as you can and we'll tell you later if it's enough."

People must know where you want to go if you expect them to help you get there. Continual communication and reinforcement of your goals and targets through all-hands meetings, newsletters, coffee pot conversations, presentations, and staff meetings are essential if you want the maximum productivity and support from the people in your organization. This is an area in which women have had a lot of practice. The communication skills women have had to use to coordinate the family unit work just as well in coordinating the work unit.

DILBERT reprinted by permission of United Feature Syndicate, Inc.

Constant communication is essential, especially if times are bad, such as during periods of downsizing or uncertainty, such as during a merger or acquisition. People will always tend to assume the worst during hard times — that they are next on the layoff list, that they are not seen as valued, or that their jobs are in constant jeopardy — unless you communicate something else to them.

People must know where you want to go if you expect them to help you get there.

If you fail to communicate fully, openly, and honestly with your employees, you run the risk of losing the best ones, as they can most easily find jobs elsewhere. If you must lay off or downsize, it is far better to do it in a single wave, identify the people who are impacted all at once, and assure the others that their jobs are secure. How the released employees are treated will have a major impact on the morale of the remaining employees. They should be treated with dignity and respect, and every attempt should be made to help them find employment elsewhere. Many companies will invest in firms to counsel and assist the departing employees in constructing their resumes and finding new employment. This investment pays off, not only in the firm's image in the marketplace, but in the morale of the "survivors," as well.

Delivering key messages personally ensures that the data are clear and unfiltered. Keep key messages few.

Several times a year, it is a good idea to have all-hands meetings, where key messages are personally delivered to all of the employees in a specific department or geographic area. I personally do this and have found that as the organizations that I manage have grown larger, it becomes more difficult, but even more necessary. Getting to hear key messages and direction firsthand has a very positive and motivational impact on people. In fact, I have actually been able to measure increases in performance, determined through revenue gains, in the time frames directly following these events.

While preparing communications to employees, it is important to ask what are the *few* key messages. It is far better to have three or four key messages or goals that are shared by all employees than to have a mish-mash of messages that are so many and so confusing that no one can remember the "nuggets." Communications, especially to large groups, are most effective when they are clear, concise, and consistent. Ronald Reagan was a master at this. He didn't alter his message or his key themes the entire time he was in public office. Everyone knew who he was and what he stood for, and his clarity and consistency allowed him to marshal the support of large numbers of people.

General Bruce Clark once said, "A unit does well in those things that its commander emphasizes." Know what you want to emphasize and communicate it clearly and effectively.

Communication is a key component of leadership. Women can use their natural focus on feelings, people, and relationships to their advantage to build partnerships with employees, peers, and clients. They just need to be aware of possible reactions to differing styles and be flexible enough to adjust when needed.

COMMUNICATING WITH YOURSELF — DEALING WITH EMOTIONAL EROSION

The constant challenging of women's credentials and competence by our society is exhausting for most women.

Many women become worn-down, burned-out, or just plain tired from the erosion, over time, of having to defend their positions and reprove their competencies. It's the little things that happen at the office, at business functions, and while on travel that add up over time — the personal comment, the innuendo that you're not really in your position because you earned it, the implication that even if you are really in the position, you still don't have the stature of men in the same job.

Often, women are assumed to be in much lower positions than they really are — not because of anything they say or wear or the way they conduct themselves — just because they are women. Other times, their authority or position is challenged by those who have no business challenging it. What's so frustrating about this behavior is that it's virtually inescapable. It invades every part of a woman's life.

Consider the emotional wear and tear resulting from the following cocktail party exchanges:

> *Often, when I attend business functions, my husband will accompany me. Almost without exception, if we are at a cocktail party where we don't know most of the people, they assume my husband is the attendee and I am the "spouse." Unbelievably, this has even happened at my company's internal events. Each time it occurs, my husband patiently explains that I am the business principal and he is the spouse. It wouldn't be so bad if it only happened occasionally, but it happens almost every time.*

Or this one:

> *At one cocktail party preceding a high tech awards event, I was very frustrated when twice in one evening, by two different men, I was asked what I did for my company. Both times, I explained that I was vice president of operations. Mind you, these men are in the same industry I am, so there was no problem with semantics. Both men, independent of each other said, "Oh, you're in sales." Each time I explained that no, while I had people who developed business who worked for me, I ran the several hundred person organization that actually delivered the ser-*

vice to the customer, usually software development or systems engineering. One man asked me a second time how many people worked for me. When I reiterated that it was over 750, he replied, "That's a lot of salespeople!" While I struggled to maintain my composure, what flashed through my mind was a vision of the painting, "The Scream." I know why she's screaming!

Here's another erosive incident that happened to a friend of mine:

One woman who is a partner in a "Big Six" accounting firm was telling me about their annual partner's meeting where all the partners gather for a few days, in casual attire, to have a series of meetings. Because of the length of the meeting and the fact that all of the firm's partners are gathered in one place, many partners bring their administrative assistants, armed with laptops, so that business continues even while they are away from the office. This particular female partner was standing in a group of male partners by the baggage claim at the airport. One of the partners from another out-of-town location came over to say hello to one of the men in the group. Seeing the woman in the group, the man said to his friend, "Oh, I see you brought your secretary." The man was mortified and hurried to introduce his peer. Thinking that this woman was perhaps one of a handful of female partners in the firm, I asked her how many female partners there were. She said, "Oh, a couple of hundred."

Another woman tells of an incident where she traveled to a city in the U.K. to conduct negotiations for her firm:

I arrived first at the conference room where the meeting was to be held. Shortly thereafter, one of the men from the other company arrived. He promptly began to give me instructions on the number of copies to be made for the meeting, as well as his desire for coffee. Somewhat taken

Edvard Munch, Geschrei (The Scream), Rosenwald Collection, © 1995 Board of Trustees, National Gallery of Art, Washington, D.C. Reprinted with permission.

I KNOW WHY SHE'S SCREAMING!

aback, I introduced myself and let him know that as soon as someone showed up who provided administrative support, I would pass his requirements on to him or her. Even after I introduced myself, gave him my title, and explained what I did, he still didn't seem to understand that we were peers.

Here's a situation in one woman's own office:

I had just moved to an area that was considerably colder than anywhere I had previously lived. One morning, it was well below zero outside. Being a Floridian, I considered this life threatening and got dressed with the weather as my main concern. Not having bought a real winter coat suitable to that area, I decided that I should wear my mink coat to work. While not really practical, it was warm. It would work. I arrived at the office very early — only a handful of people were there, and it was very quiet. As I walked down the hall to my office, I passed a group of a half-dozen men, two of whom worked for me. Not wanting to interrupt their conversation, I just smiled and nodded and kept walking. As I got past them, I heard one man, whom I had never seen before, say, "Now there goes a secretary with a sugar daddy." Imagine my surprise, when a couple of hours later, the same man showed up at my office. He was my 10 o'clock appointment. He was asking me to fund his project. Imagine his surprise when I closed my door for our meeting and he saw my coat and realized I was the one he was referring to earlier.

Or this travel situation that often happens to me and many other women I know:

I fly a lot in my business, and I'm usually dressed in a business suit when I do. I was surprised on one flight when a gentleman asked me to hang up his coat. After my

*initial shock, I realized he thought I was the flight atten-
dant. On another flight, a man asked me to get him a
drink. On yet another flight, a man asked me to put his
bags in the overhead bin for him. This one was especially
absurd, as I'm very petite and can reach the bin only by
standing on a seat. What made this whole thing odd, is
that sometimes it happened, and sometimes it didn't. After much puzzling, I finally figured out that every time I
wore a navy blue suit on an airplane, someone assumed I
was a flight attendant! I've found that it's just easier to
plan what I wear on a flight than to explain that I don't
work for the airline just because I'm female and wearing
a blue suit.*

Sometimes these things happen even when you're the client, as
told by this woman:

*In one job I had, I had several field offices reporting in to
me. At one point, I was evaluating which offices to keep
open and which ones to close. In one particular instance,
we were at a unique location that was very expensive compared to the prevailing real estate prices in other parts of
the city. I made a special trip to that site with two of the
men who worked for me to assess the value-added by the
unique location. We had a meeting with a man from the
property management company in a small conference room.
Even though my title showed clearly that I was the senior-
most person at the meeting, the man from the property
company ignored me to the point of turning his back on
me for most of his presentation. Often during the presentation, the two men with me reminded the property manager that it was my decision to renew the lease, not theirs.
He continued to ignore me, up to and including the wrap-
up, where he said, "Well, gentlemen, what do you think?"
He never did get it.*

It even happens outside of business, and it even happens by other women:

> *A friend of mine held a board position for a local theater. He had elected to take an overseas assignment and was forced to resign from the board. The board asked him to recommend his replacement. He and I were peers. He recommended me and assured me it was a "rubber stamp" procedure for me to be approved. A woman from the theater board called to set up a meeting with me. Assuming it was about the board position, I made time to see her, even though it was inconvenient at the time she wanted. One of the responsibilities of the board was to raise money, so I had a check prepared from my company as a donation to the theater and as my first official "board act." The woman was extremely late for our meeting, and I had just about given up on her when she finally showed. Because it was really her meeting, I let her set the agenda. After a long time beating around the bush and getting nowhere, I finally asked her very directly about my confirmation for the board seat. She seemed shocked by my question, and said, "Oh good heavens. We would never ask someone like you to be on the board. You're not nearly senior enough. We've asked 'John Doe' to fill the open seat. I'm just here because I thought you might be able to help us find someone in your organization who would be willing to make a donation." "John Doe" worked for me, two levels down. I was his boss' boss.*

The amazing thing about all of these situations is that the data were available for the "offenders" to process. Titles were presented, name tags were worn, corner offices were occupied. But the parties involved had their own paradigms of the jobs women *should* be in and were not going to allow themselves to be swayed by data, regardless of the number of times it was presented — and regardless of how much business or how many donations it cost them. While the stories may change over time, new behaviors will result in new stories and new erosion.

The most damaging aspect of this type of behavior is the long-term effect it can have on the female recipients. Many women will take these comments in, stew over them, and, over time, allow them to impact their confidence and self-esteem. The women who allow themselves to believe that this erosive behavior is exhibited by these others on purpose — with the primary intention of hurting them — are making the choice to be hurt by it.

If your lawn were eroding, you would take action. Take action, also, against emotional erosion. Take charge of how you interpret the message.

If your lawn were being eroded by outside forces, you wouldn't stand back and watch and feel hurt. You would take action. You would plant grass, build a retaining wall — whatever it took. Women should do likewise for the erosion of their positions, power, or self-esteem. When this erosive behavior occurs, consider one or more of the following:

- **Ignore it altogether.** Maggie Bedrosian, author of *Speak Like a Pro* and *Life is More than Your To Do List*, says she tries to "ignore five annoying things a day." I know I have days when five is not enough to ignore. But, her excellent point is, why waste precious energy on things you cannot change?
- **Try to change your belief system.** Rather than subscribe to the fact that others are trying to hurt you, believe that they are ignorant or unaware. It's not likely that the men at the cocktail party were trying to insult or hurt me, especially considering that I was in a position to give them rather large subcontracts. They were simply unaware of how annoying their

behavior was. I, on the other hand, had a choice of letting their behavior ruin my evening or understanding their lack of awareness.

- **Point out the offending behavior.** Regardless of whether you believe the behavior is based on ignorance or is intentional, sometimes it is helpful to point it out to the offending parties. After all, if no one ever tells them, they will never know — or if it's intentional, they will always get away with it. If you do, make sure it is in a nonemotional, nondefensive way and is focused on the behavior, not the person. Use "I" language rather than "you" language. Put things in terms that explain how you felt or the impact it had on you at the time. I know many women who constantly complain about the same people over and over but tell everyone *but* the person who can do something about it. On the flip side of this, pick your battles carefully. If you take on everyone who offends you, you will get little else done and will probably be seen as a "whiner." Make certain when you bring this up to someone, that it is worth your investment of time and energy to work through it.

How you communicate with yourself is as important to your success as how you communicate with others. Find your own way to minimize the emotional wear and tear that results from this erosion of the soul. Take charge of how you interpret the messages, and learn what it takes for you to "survive gracefully."

Chapter Eleven

Power — What It Is, How to Use It

Nobody gives you power — you take it.

-Jock Ewing to Bobby Ewing on "Dallas"

In corporate terms, power is a
useful tool and a legitimate objective.

-Paul Stern

TYPES OF POWER

There are many different types of power that combine to form the total amount of influence, or control, a person exercises. This explains why two people seemingly at the same level of responsibility have vastly different levels of power.

Webster defines power as "the ability or capacity to exercise control." This is true in business as well — those with great power exercise great control. But why do these people have the power they have in the first place? How did they get it? How do they keep it? And why can two people seemingly at the same level of responsibility have vastly different levels of power? I believe there are many different types of power that combine to form the total amount of influence, or control, a person exercises. Let's discuss the main types:

- Personal power
- Position power
- Expertise or knowledge power
- Referent power

Personal power. Personal power contains many components, one of which is charisma. We've all met people who change the dynamics of a group just by walking into a room. They are able to move people into action just by the sheer force of their personalities. Most people with charisma are born with it. They are good communicators, polished speakers, and present themselves well. They make excellent leaders and politicians. They have an energy about themselves, and a vitality that is contagious to others around them. They are upbeat, positive, and motivational.

> *One man, who was my boss' boss, was the most charismatic man for whom I have ever worked. I'll call him "Greg." Greg was like a breath of fresh air coming into the room. I knew him for years and never knew him to have a bad day or be anything but upbeat and positive. He was the best salesperson I've ever known. I never saw him lose a deal, whether it was negotiating with a client or a job candidate. When we had disgruntled employees, we used to send them to Greg's office — that had a nice couch for visitors — to let Greg talk to them. He always made them forget what was bothering them and feel happy to be a part of the company. We used to call this a "couch job." No matter who it was, Greg never failed to boost*

their morale. His "couch jobs" saved a lot of employees who otherwise would have left the company.

While I don't believe that charisma can be learned, I do believe that people who want to be more charismatic can adopt some elements of this behavior and raise their "charisma quotient" above what it is now. If you are concerned that you are not particularly charismatic, try reading some of the motivational or self-help books on positive imaging or adopting a more positive attitude. Or look into seminars on the same topics. Learn also how to communicate more positively and more assertively (see Chapter Ten).

Personal power can also be increased by leveraging these other components:

- Experience with and command of your subject matter
- Working your contacts and network
- Having good communication skills that cause people to listen to you or read your work
- Having self-confidence
- Listening to others — being approachable
- Following up — letting others see that you do bring things to closure
- Speaking up — sharing ideas, causing thought, influencing action.
- Keeping others informed of what you are doing
- Getting feedback and finding out if the path you are on is consistent with others' thinking
- Continuously learning — from reading, observing others, taking classes
- Paying attention to detail — finding typos, returning phone calls, being sensitive to the tone of your messages

Part of how well your "power package" is viewed has to do with how well you use things at your disposal — titles, perks, facilities — to increase your image and people's perception of your status or position.

Position power. Another kind of power, that is far more tangible, is the power of position. Managers have certain power over their subordinates simply because they control their assignments, raises, and promotions. They have certain power in their organizations because of the number of people they manage and the size of the budgets they control. A manager's "position" power is usually proportional to the impact that manager's organization has on the bottom line in that particular company. Again, however, you will find examples of people with similar positions in companies who have widely varying amounts of power. This can be attributed to the fact that the whole "package" that person presents is more powerful than the package the other person presents. Position power is increased by:

- Being in charge — using your authority and responsibility to make decisions with respect to people, budgets, assets
- Having a vision — and reinforcing it at every opportunity
- Putting the right people in key jobs and then delegating to them
- Knowing when *not* to decide — knowing when to follow your   instincts and decide when a change feels more "right"
- Gaining consensus — soliciting ideas, working through issues together, arriving at issues together, making informed decisions when consensus cannot be reached
- Getting results
- Continually improving — creating sound practices, being willing to change, being willing to reengineer
- Being corporate — being willing to step outside your own organization to see the larger picture and do what's right

- Being direct — telling it like it is, admitting mistakes
- Reinforcing teamwork — getting people to work together, establishing participation and commitment
- Empowering others and making sure they have the visibility they need to "feel powerful"
- Being unique — accepting responsibility as a role model

Expertise or knowledge power. Expertise, or knowledge power, comes into play when you are one of a few, or the only one, who knows how to do something that others want done. It can be as simple as the secretary who is the only one who knows how to run the fax machine, to the knowledge worker who is the only one who can fix the client's computer program before the contract is canceled.

During the oil crisis in the 1970s, there were several key people at this particular oil company who had the expertise to find the oil reserves that were not currently being worked. Suddenly, we needed all the oil we could get our hands on, and we needed it now. Most of these people were very junior — engineers and geologists. Many of them worked through the night, night after night. It was fun to watch the senior executives hovering over them asking what they could do. I lost count of the number of vice presidents and division managers who made late night runs to Burger King to keep these junior people fed. For those few brief weeks, the engineers and geologists could have named their price.

Having the power to do something no one else can do does make you powerful in certain situations — those situations where others need you — but be cautious with this, as sometimes you will need those same people to get your job done. Knowledge power can be increased by:

- Staying current in your area of expertise

- Developing new areas of expertise as technology or your company changes
- Making others aware of your talents and skills
- Being accessible
- Being willing to help out in a crisis

Referent power. Referent power is the power that comes from a clear, consistent set of values. The Pope is a good example of an individual with values that never waver. He will give the same speeches year after year, all over the world, clearly and consistently. People always know what he believes, and it makes people believe in him. When your values and beliefs are so strong and consistent, when you can set clear goals and direction and never waver, people will follow you, even if they don't always agree with your message.

This is powerful stuff for managers of people. It seems so easy to do, but many people in positions of leadership fail to grasp it. In his 1988 campaign, Vice President Bush was remembered most for his campaign pledge, "Read my lips. No new taxes." Those few words carried a powerful message and brought the house down that night in New Orleans. Just two years later, Bush caved to members of his staff and cabinet and agreed to raise taxes. That was the beginning of the end. The voters did not forgive him for this change in direction, regardless of how right it might have been for the country, and he lost his re-election bid.

Referent power can be leveraged by:

- Having easily identifiable values
- Having a clear message and a *few* key points
- Communicating those key points clearly and succinctly (they should fit on a small, laminated card)
- Never wavering, never compromising

A survey of members of the International Women's Forum, an international networking organization for prominent women leaders, showed that women are much more likely to use the attributes of personal power — charisma, networking, communicating — as opposed to power based on "organizational position, title, or the ability to reward and punish." I believe that the more you can leverage all four types of power, the better your "package" will be.

HANDLING POWER

The way one deals with the trappings that accompany power has a major impact on the way one is viewed by others and, therefore, the amount of control, or real power, that one has over others.

Part of how well your "package" is viewed has to do with how well you use all the things at your disposal — titles, perks, facilities — to increase your image and people's perception of your status or position. President Nixon was perceived as using the trappings of his office — airplanes, helicopters, and yachts, among other things — to such an extent that his was dubbed the "Imperial Presidency." When Ford took over as president, his staff made a major effort to downplay the majesty of the office and make him look like a "regular Joe." They went so far as to stage photo opportunities with him making toast in the White House kitchen and playing with his dog on the White House lawn.

Clearly, the way one deals with the trappings that accompany power has a major impact on the way one is viewed by others and, therefore, the amount of control, or real power, that one has over others. Many people who have real power understand the care they must take when exercising it — care not to rule so heavy-handedly as to stifle the creativity or energy of the people in their organizations.

I was writing a speech for the chairman of our corpora-
tion. Before my work got to him, it was reviewed by sev-

eral members of his staff. Each time, it came back with heavy red marks all over it. Each time, I would make the corrections and send it on to the next person. Finally, I felt it was ready to be read by the chairman. When it came back, at first I thought he had no comments. Then immediately, I thought, no, he must not have read it. Upon closer inspection, I noticed that he had several comments penciled lightly in the margins. He had taken great care not to be heavy handed in the way he reviewed it. Later, I had the opportunity to ask him why he used pencil, instead of red pen like the other reviewers. He said he felt that red pen from the chairman would be too intimidating. Pencil made the point, but much more subtly.

"You can tell how secure a person is by the way he or she handles power. Really secure people handle it well. Insecure people abuse it."

-Former White House Employee

A woman I know who used to work at the White House said to me once, *"You can tell how secure a person is by the way he or she handles power. Really secure people handle it well. Insecure people abuse it."* I thought about what she said and tried to think of some exceptions, but I couldn't. This ties in well with the good boss/bad boss syndrome. The bad bosses abuse their power over their subordinates by treating them poorly and failing to take responsibility for their own shortcomings — also signs of insecurity. Many managers who actually feel powerless attempt to mask this by adopting petty or dictatorial styles and, in turn, making their employees feel powerless.

A splendid example of a blatant abuse of power comes from a woman I used to work with in a Fortune 500 company. We were both vice presidents — I was in an opera-

tions job, and she was in a staff job. For some reason, she decided that she deserved a car and driver — something that simply did not accompany our pay grade, or even the one above ours. She decided that she would create her own perk — by insisting that one of her employees drive her around in her own car, during business hours and outside of business hours! This young man, who had an advanced degree and aspired to do great things in the company, was forced to chauffeur her around day and night and to sit and wait for her while she attended meetings or dinners. I can only assume that the reason this young man did not complain was that he feared for his job — this occurred during the period of massive downsizing in many large corporations.

Many truly powerful people treat everyone they meet — from CEOs to cleaning personnel — with exactly the same dignity and respect.

I can think of many, many more abuses of power by bosses over their subordinates — cases where the manager disclosed intensely personal information about the employee to others, where the manager forced the employee to perform personal tasks for him, or where the manager verbally abused or sexually harassed the employee just because he or she could. These abuses of power are horrendously demotivating and do not serve the employees or the corporation well.

Good managers and leaders use their power to get positive things done. They use it to motivate employees, make money for the company, and produce results. There is certainly nothing wrong with using all of the perks and insisting on all of the benefits associated with your position, but it is never appropriate to abuse or demean your employees. It is particularly interesting to note that many truly powerful people treat everyone they meet — from CEOs to cleaning personnel — with exactly the same dignity and respect. When you are truly comfortable with yourself, it is much easier to be comfortable with everyone around you — regardless of their position.

It's an interesting phenomenon that the higher you progress up the corporate ladder, the more position power you will have; but you will also have less direct control over the people doing the real work. You must rely on those below you for your success, never quite knowing the whole story — having to trust others for information. Paul Stern, former CEO of Northern Telecom, writes in his book *Straight to the Top*, "As you go up the ladder, while you exercise and enjoy your power, you must simultaneously develop a tolerance for ambiguity, uncertainty, and the ability to live with a lot of loose ends."

WOMEN'S TENDENCY TO GIVE POWER AWAY

Powerful people should use powerful language that shows that they are certain about their ability to contribute and get things done.

Because of the way they've been socialized, many women believe that power is "corrupt" or "evil." Power, in and of itself, is neither good nor bad. It just is. The abuse or misuse of power, however, can be considered corrupt or evil. So, we should learn to use the power at our disposal from our positions, personalities, expertise, and values but not to misuse it or abuse it.

Women should use their titles, accept their perks, and let their staffs take care of all they can for them. Women should insist on being called "Dr." or "Ms." when their colleagues are addressed similarly, use their offices when negotiating megadeals, and use their cars when traveling to power lunches. For too long, women have given all this away in order to accommodate those around them; but when they give up each of these things, they give away a piece of their power and diminish their effectiveness versus their colleagues who "take" power, Jock Ewing style. One female consulting partner tells how, after the fact, she realized she was giving away power — and that in the end, it really did matter.

> *When I first made partner, I found that I worked on a number of engagements with other partners. The paperwork that we filled out for each engagement forced us to list one partner as the lead partner, even though we might share the work. The other partners with whom I worked wanted to be listed as lead, even if we were in a shared role. Not being one to haggle over who gets credit, I acquiesced in most instances. At the end of the year, we filled out our portion of our annual performance appraisal forms. These forms were important, because they, in part, determined our bonus levels. When I saw the partner form for the first time, I was shocked to see that one way in which we were measured was on the number of engagements where we were listed as lead. Even though the company stressed teamwork, the measurement systems stressed individual accomplishments. Apparently, the more experienced partners had learned to "game" the system by getting all the individual credit they could. I needed to learn to get credit for my work as well.*

Women also tend to render themselves powerless by their use of language. In Deborah Tannen's book, *You Just Don't Understand*, she discusses how, according to men, women use powerless language and may not even be aware of it. Women are very conscious of how their words affect others and often are indirect in order to allow others to save face. Women's language is often sprinkled with conciliatory words or phrases like "please," "thank you," or "I'm sorry" to soften messages or requests. Many women sound unsure and tentative by ending sentences with such phrases as "Isn't it?" or "Don't you think?" Often women will start a sentence with, "Correct me if I'm wrong," knowing full well they are not wrong. In the end, what women view as polite, men often view as weak. Additionally, the fact that women do not jockey for the one-up position the way men do, causes men to view women as "one-down," or less powerful.

Women also typically wait for things to come to them, rather than make things happen. A good example is work assignments or clients. Most women wait to be asked if they want a certain job or client assignment, while most men will see an assignment they want and aggressively go after it. This hesitation by women to "take" what they want is often viewed by men as a weakness.

Powerful people should use powerful language that shows that they are certain about their abilities to contribute and get things done. They don't need the approval or seconding of their opinions in order to be sure they are right. Being confidant and sure offends no one. Women are already adept at adjusting their behavior in order to "connect" with others. Matching what is viewed by others as powerful, or at least neutral, language is merely one more way to connect — only this time in the business world.

BIOLOGY AND POWER

Scientific research in men and women has determined that the higher the testosterone level, the higher the aggression. It has also shown that women injected with testosterone will exhibit "male-like" or more aggressive behavior.

In our society, women have historically had lower status than men, partly because money contributes to power, and women have been in low paying, or even no-paying jobs. Too, women have not joined in the one-up games and power struggles in which men routinely engage. One might question the reason for this second factor — women's lack of aggressive jockeying for position and power — and one might receive the answer that this is attributable to the many differences between men and women.

One of the interesting facts that has come out of the cognitive brain research on men and women is that the male hormone testosterone is largely the cause of aggressive behavior in men. Scientific research in men and women has determined that the higher the testosterone level, the higher the aggression. It has also shown that women injected with testosterone will exhibit more aggressive (or "male-like") behavior.

This becomes even more fascinating when you consider the fact that more than 40 million American women— the baby boomers — will reach menopause in the next 20 years. With this change, they will experience a major drop in their bodies' production of the female hormone estrogen, and with that, the "unmasking" of their natural levels of testosterone. In her book *Office Biology*, Edith Weiner addresses what this means to our current power structure. "Their testosterone, clearly linked to aggressiveness and now less tempered by high estrogen levels, has led middle-aged women in many societies to gain greater influence.... As we look forward to a bumper crop of mid-life women, we can look forward to a major power surge." At the same time that these 40 million women experience their "power surge," approximately the same number of men will experience the decreasing testosterone levels associated with their own aging process — a power decline, if you will. This should make for interesting times, indeed!

Chapter Twelve

Negotiating Skills

*It is the nature of men to be bound by the
benefits they confer as much as by those they receive.*

-Niccolo Machiavelli

NEGOTIATING TIPS

**With scarce resources and never enough time or money, today's
managers must negotiate for nearly everything. Fortunately for
women, they're used to it.**

In these days of lean organizations and cross-functional
workgroups, knowing how to negotiate is becoming increasingly
important. Managers must negotiate for budgets, resources, priority
programs, office space — almost everything! Few things in business
are done without some level of negotiation. If you have contact with
suppliers or clients, you probably have occasion to negotiate with
them as well — for price, delivery, quality, and any number of other
things.

Women have had extensive experience in negotiating because they have had to accomplish most tasks in their lives with little real power. Women's experiences in nonprofit and charity organizations have taught them to get funding, resources, and assistance with nothing other than their powers of negotiation. Women tend to be good negotiators because they look at the big picture, don't negotiate with their egos, and don't get hung up on small details where they don't agree.

In Deborah Tannen's book, *You Just Don't Understand*, she explains how men view life as a series of one-up contests, where they are always vying for position, while women will make great efforts to "connect" with others, even if it means putting themselves in a "one-down" position to do so. Being willing and able to subjugate their egos in order to connect with the person with whom they are negotiating is a great advantage for women. It is amazing what you can learn from your negotiating partner when you can connect. (I use the word partner rather than opponent because if you weren't working toward the same goal, you wouldn't be negotiating.)

A factor that makes negotiating easy is that while the parties may want the same end result (e.g., a signed contract), their interests in the contract are rarely the same. As the buyer, I want quality products on time. As the seller, I want cash. The details of the product delivery will be much more important to the buyer and much more of a negotiating point for the seller. On the other hand, the payment terms are probably much more important to the seller.

Do your homework. In a negotiation, take the time and make the effort to understand those two or three points on which the other party simply cannot yield and determine the same about your position. Do your internal homework as well. If you are not the final authority on all matters you are negotiating, such as payment terms, try to get certain limits preapproved, so that you have the flexibility to "give" in areas where you can. Chances are, when you determine the nonnegotiable points for both parties, they will not be the same points. Everything else is negotiable. When you are ready to negotiate, focus the presentation of your position on the benefits to your partner, the trade-offs, and why your solution is win-win.

Gain an understanding of the other party. Establishing rapport with your partners, getting to know them, and understanding their issues prior to the negotiations will enable you to negotiate better. Go to dinner the night before, and learn about them personally — their jobs, their companies, how they are measured, what their priorities are. Is the company strapped for cash? Will a delay in your product delivery cost them an important customer? Could favorable payment terms mean the difference to them between staying in business or going belly-up? If you understand how their business is doing and what motivates them personally, it will then be easier to determine what their sticking points are and where they might be willing to yield.

Sometimes, the other party will ask for something that, to you, seems outrageous — perhaps a lot of extra work at no extra cost. When this happens, try to figure out what they are really after. Do they really need all the extra work they asked for? Or is there one small piece that they *must* have, and they don't realize it can be done without the other? If you can really get to the heart of what they want, you will often find that what is high value to the other party is actually low cost or low effort for you. When this happens, you can give them something very valuable and, therefore, be in a position for them to do likewise for you.

Be considerate, polite, and honest. In the old style of negotiating, opponents used to work at intimidating each other and trying to anger each other. If you are trying to have a win-win negotiation, making your negotiating partner uncomfortable will not assist you in getting to a win-win solution. In today's world, with partnerships and alliances often defining success, you cannot afford to alienate someone who could later be a strategic supplier or customer. Women have an edge here. While they have often been called excessively polite in business, this is actually helpful in negotiations, as long as they don't get so polite that they cave on an issue of importance.

Be a good communicator. Make certain that you state your objectives clearly and listen closely while your partner states his or hers. Summarize often where you are in the negotiation to make certain that things on which you think you have agreement are really resolved. "Let's see where we are. You need delivery earlier than our standard delivery time but are not in a position to pay us up front to expedite because you are short on cash until your customer pays you. I can't dip below my margin target, but I don't get measured until the end of the quarter. Can you pay us the expedite fee at the back end, before the end of the quarter?"

Think creatively. Often, the solution can be found if you come at the problem from a different angle. Women are sometimes accused of doing this in arguments — trying to make the same point from a different angle — but it is actually helpful in negotiations to keep trying angles until you find one that clicks with your partner. Helping your partner see your side, and why you can't yield on a particular point, will enhance understanding. Also, thinking of nontraditional ways to solve your partner's problems may mean the difference between a deal that goes through and one that goes south.

There's a very funny, but true, story about how one man thought creatively during negotiations in Japan after World War II.

> *I was a young lieutenant in the U.S. Army, stationed in Japan in 1956. Following the war, we had negotiated something with the Japanese called the Master Labor Agreement, that had terms and conditions regarding how Japanese employees would be treated. At this particular base, we had a large mess hall that was staffed primarily by Japanese women, who were, of course, covered under this Labor Agreement. One of the terms in the agreement was that each woman was entitled to two days a month of "physiological leave," supposedly during her menstrual cycle.*

Well, what happened as a result is that the women would just disappear without warning two days a month, and the sergeant who ran the mess hall couldn't plan the staffing. This went on for awhile, and the sergeant told me he just couldn't deal with this uncertainty in staffing — it was making his job impossible. I told the sergeant and his Japanese interpreter to figure out a solution before the problem got any worse. The next day, the interpreter came to me and asked me to trust him. He thought he'd worked it out in his mind, but he wanted to convene the women and see if they were amenable to his proposed solution. He didn't want to tell me what the solution was until he had proposed it.

We convened the women and the interpreter began to speak to them in Japanese. He was apparently telling them that we had a problem with their "physiological leave," as you could see that they were unhappy. He then went into an explanation of his solution, and the women perked up and finally broke out in applause. Happy, but not sure why, I asked him what he had proposed. Well, he said, the women didn't really need the two days off for their menstrual cycles, but they had gotten used to having the free time. He told them that they could continue to have the time off for their cycles, as long as we got to tell them when their "cycles" were. By thinking outside the box, the young interpreter had come up with a win-win solution.

Be willing to say no. Not everyone cares about whether you see the negotiation as win-win. Some negotiating partners will offer you terms that are unacceptable or solutions that are untenable. Do not be afraid to say no. Remember, negotiations are give and take. Sometimes your partner must also give. Also, do not be afraid to walk away from the table if the deal is not a good one for you or your company, and your negotiating partner will not yield. Some deals are just not meant to be.

Don't get emotional. Sometimes, negotiations can get heated, especially if both parties have a lot at stake. The other party may intentionally say or do things to upset or inflame you. Don't buy into this. Once you lose your composure, you have lost your edge.

Don't take things personally. Not everyone cares about win-win negotiating. Some people want to win at all costs. Many old-style negotiators were trained to use intimidation and insults as negotiating tools. If you encounter people like this, don't take anything in the negotiations personally. They are merely using the tools they have learned. If your negotiating partner gets too personal, you can, however, request that you keep the negotiations focused on the business at hand.

Make sure you keep your word. Your word in a negotiation should be binding. If you agree to something and then later renege, no one will want to deal with you anymore — your business dealings have lost the element of trust. Sometimes you make a mistake when you commit to something. If that is the case, and it is too significant for you or your company to let it go, you must explain the situation and correct it at once. Be willing to compensate the other party in some way for allowing you to modify your existing agreement.

Other times, you will be in a position to step in and complete negotiations begun by someone else or to implement a contract negotiated by others. In these cases, your predecessor's word or the company's contract is the same as *your* word. This story illustrates how important that is to the other party.

> *I had just taken over as the general manager of a small software firm. My predecessor had been fired, and things were in a real mess. After visiting all the key clients, I began to visit the key partners we had. There were several strategic alliances and joint software development efforts in process. One, in particular, seemed key to our efforts and I set up a meeting with the president of the company and our liaison. They suggested they come to our office, and we agreed.*

In preparation for the meeting, I studied the contracts we had with them for joint development and software licenses. They seemed fair and balanced. I talked to my senior staff about the agreement, and they agreed that it was important to our success in many of our target markets. I looked forward to the meeting.

The day of the meeting, the two gentlemen from our partner company entered our conference room looking grim. My financial controller and I looked at each other in surprise — we were expecting a happy meeting, primarily centered around getting to know each other and cementing our relationship. The gentlemen began by telling us they had consulted their attorney and were beginning legal proceedings against our company. Taken aback, I asked them to explain to me, the "new guy," what the problem was. They proceeded to tell me how my predecessor had violated our agreement in many ways, and how he had refused to negotiate with them on several fronts. Because my predecessor did not live up to the contract, they expected me not to, either. They were at their wit's end and saw no recourse but to sue.

I grabbed a magic marker, went over to the flip chart, and said, "Tell me all your issues." One by one, they listed them. Immediately, I was able to see that there wasn't a single one we couldn't work through. Basically, we were in violation of our own contract, and they wanted us to fix it — and fix it now. The controller and I went through each issue with them, bringing in subject matter experts as needed. We negotiated a plan for how we would get back on track on each item.

Neither my staff nor I had any idea that we were so far off the mark. They believed they were implementing the contract because they were doing what my predecessor had told them to do. I believed we were implementing it be-

213

cause they told me we were. It was a long and exhausting day, but we managed to convince our partner company that we were sincere in our efforts to live up to the letter of the contract. They canceled their efforts with their attorney and took us to dinner to celebrate our new relationship. Even though several of the principals involved have moved on to other companies, we developed such a solid relationship of trust and respect, that we still keep up with each other years later.

If you reach an impasse in your negotiation, try one or more of the following before throwing in the towel:

- **Take a break.** Sometimes, both parties get fatigued or stressed and can no longer think creatively. Take a walk. Go to lunch. Go to dinner. Reconvene the next day with a clear head.
- **Stress the positive.** Summarize all the areas where you do agree. It may make you realize that you are 90% of the way there and give you new energy and hope that an agreement can be reached.
- **Summarize the areas where you still disagree.** This is the inverse of the point above, but sometimes realizing that you are only apart on one or two issues gives you new impetus to keep going.
- **Summarize your partner's position.** Clarify what you believe to be your negotiating partner's position. Sometimes you are wrong, and this new information can cause movement in the negotiation again.
- **Get a third party's opinion.** Sometimes having a neutral party hear both positions, as well as where and why you are stuck, can be helpful. They may suggest another approach or a solution that neither of you had considered.

NEGOTIATING STYLES

Sometimes your negotiations are stymied not by real issues, but by style differences. Knowing your partners' styles can be helpful in understanding how they should be approached.

Sometimes what makes negotiating difficult is not a difference in objectives, but rather a difference in style. Perhaps you are very analytical and matter-of-fact, and your partner is emotional and prone to take everything you say personally. Often, knowing your partner's style will be helpful in understanding how he or she should be approached. There are many sources of information on personality and preference styles that might be helpful. One good source is a set of audiocassettes by Roger Dawson, *The Secrets of Power Negotiating*, that has two modules on personality types. Another good source is the Otto Kroeger, Janet Thuesen book, *Type Talk at Work*. This book outlines the Myers-Briggs preference types and how they interact. (See also Chapter Ten.)

Whatever source you use, it is helpful for you to understand that when someone's style is in opposition to yours, you must take care to communicate with them in a manner in which you will be successful. People often make the mistake of thinking that everyone views the world the way that they do, but nothing could be further from the truth.

For an analytical, matter-of-fact, to-the-point person, the more intuitive, feeling person looks like an emotional blow-hard who never gets to the point and wastes their time. To the feeling, intuitive person, the analytical, matter-of-fact person looks cold, unfeeling, and abrupt. Without understanding these differences, one runs the risk of offending the negotiating partner by talking too little, talking too much, not warming them up, spending too much up-front time socializing, or any number of style faux pas.

I once had a peer with whom I normally did not interface a lot, but due to circumstances that were unusual, we were on a project together. This project was fraught with problems, some of which my organization had to solve, and some of which my peer's organization had to solve. Being an engineer, when faced with a problem, I would take out a piece of paper and try to define the problem clearly. I would attempt to put boundaries around it, and then work on the possible solutions. I would then define action items for my organization, assign them, and track them. Much to my surprise, my peer had a different approach. When faced with a serious problem, he underwent a period of what someone in my organization fondly called "chasing his tail." Only after expending a certain amount of emotional energy in this exercise could he start actually solving the problem. I couldn't figure out why this man kept going to my boss telling him I was not solving the problems my organization was faced with, when I had folders of charts, graphs, action items, and schedules that proved otherwise.

Finally, after some intervention from a third party, I discovered that because of our style differences, we had a significant misunderstanding. All he saw was that I never emoted, never "chased my tail"; therefore, he couldn't believe that I was actually working the problem behind the scenes. His belief was that if I didn't emote, I either didn't know that this was a problem, or I didn't care. Once I understood this about him, I was better able to put into words my understanding of the problem and make him see that I really did grasp its severity.

The purpose in understanding your negotiating partner is to emphasize the similarities and smooth out the differences. If you take the time to understand your partners' styles, where they are coming from, and what's really important to every party, everyone can win.

Remember, if they didn't want the same thing you did, they wouldn't be negotiating.

NEGOTIATING FOR YOURSELF

We must learn that, as a rule, no one will take care of us, and no one will give us anything we don't ask for.

Because of the way they've been socialized, many women believe that someone else will look out for their salaries, their careers, and their lives. They believe that there are set rules for everything, and that the same set of rules will be applied fairly to everybody — whether they ask for consideration or not. This is simply not true.

I have seen men get more money than women for the same jobs because men ask for more. I have seen men get better relocation benefits than women at the same level because the men demanded it. For some reason, women tend to be more patient with things the way they are and less likely to force a change. Women also tend to accept initial offers more readily, without trying to negotiate an improved position for themselves.

In one management position I held, it was very easy to compare the men's and women's salaries in the technical ranks. It was also easy to see that the women did indeed make substantially less in the same jobs, with the same education and level of experience. I made a case to my human resources department regarding the inequity, and we adjusted the women's salaries — sometimes as much as 25% — to be in range with the men's.

Unfortunately, statistics show that within another 10 years, these women will fall out of range again, primarily because they don't constantly negotiate their salaries to keep up, and secondarily, because many of the people these women will encounter who will impact their salaries over time still think of men as the "breadwinners" and will tend to give the men larger increases, regardless of performance.

I still remember my shock when I was told by the vice president of human resources at one firm where I worked — when I argued that I should be brought up to the minimum salary for the job I was performing — that I "made a lot of money for a single female." Would it not be a lot of money if I were married? Or male? And what did "minimum" mean, anyway?

Women must negotiate to get their salaries up to parity with men in similar positions and keep them up where they belong. When doing so, sell your value to the company — don't emphasize issues of equity or parity.

Women should periodically benchmark their salaries and ensure that they are competitively paid. In 1995, the U.S. Labor Department reported that women have made great strides in their salaries — they now make 71% of what their male counterparts make, a 20% increase over the past 15 years. Clearly, this is not acceptable, but I've found that unless you have an extraordinary boss and a proactive human resources department, your salary will probably not be raised just because the men in your department make more for doing the same job.

A better and more effective approach is to sell an increase to your boss based on your contribution to the company. Cite specific examples of cost savings and revenue generating measures you have personally enacted, or contributed to, and the impact to the bottom line. Or illustrate the value you have added to a particular project or customer deliverable, and how it wouldn't have enjoyed nearly the success it had without your contribution. Regardless of their politics or preferences for hiring men or women, most bosses are willing to pay for value, if it can be proven to them.

In many companies, your performance appraisal rating relates to your salary increase or bonus. While most people would not hesitate to negotiate for a salary increase, many people settle for a performance rating that is less than they deserve. One woman found out how big the impact was.

> *I received my performance appraisal and was shocked that I didn't receive the highest rating. I knew what I had contributed to the business versus my peers, and I knew that if I wasn't the top performer, I was pretty close. I asked my boss what I could have done differently or better that would have given me the highest rating. I think I stumped him. He honestly didn't know what to say. I asked him to think about it, because I didn't want to be in the same situation next year. I knew the review had already made its way through the system, so I didn't hold out much hope for getting it changed, but I did want him to understand that I had expected a higher rating, based on my performance and understanding of his expectations. A few weeks later, he called me into his office and told me that after our conversation, he decided that I really did deserve the highest rating, and that he had redone the review and sent it back through the system. Much to my surprise, the new rating almost doubled my bonus!*

When negotiating salary, think in terms of total compensation and decide what is really important to you.

Another way to get your salary up, of course, is to negotiate it up during a job change. This can be a job change inside your current company or during a change of companies. When negotiating for a new position, think in terms of total compensation, and decide which aspects are most important to you. Salary may the be most important, but also consider other ways to be compensated, such as bonuses, stock options, and paid leave. Do you really require the cash flow of having all of your compensation in salary, or can some of it be deferred in these other forms?

Different companies have differing levels of flexibility. Some companies are more willing to go over the "maximum" salary for a job grade, but hold stock options and other perks very close. Other companies will not budge past a salary cap, but will be very generous with bonuses or stock. Figure out what you require in cash flow, and determine how flexible the company can be on the other aspects of compensation. You will get no consideration if you do not ask.

Every job change, even internally, is an opportunity to negotiate.

Each time you accept a new assignment or more responsibility is an opportunity for you to negotiate for something else on your wish list. When you do this, make sure you:

- Research what others are getting for similar levels of responsibility so that you know what is reasonable
- Are firm and clear about your expectations
- Ask for more than you are willing to settle for

From time to time, every company will have a project, product, or operating unit that is in serious trouble and in need of someone to "fix it." Usually, this will require short periods of intense effort and personal sacrifice, such as heavy travel, relocation, long hours, or giving up a job you really like. Sometimes, depending on how bad the situation is, the periods of sacrifice might be long. These are excellent opportunities for negotiating.

If you are fortunate enough to be considered for one of these "rescue" assignments, weigh the level of sacrifice needed to complete the task and bargain *up front* for the appropriate level of recognition from the company when it is accomplished. This could be anywhere from a bonus tied to the amount of money you saved the company, to time off, to finally getting that promotion you deserve. Get agreement up front — and get it in writing. Then do everything you said you would do, and more. If you do not perform in a superior manner in the "rescue" assignment, you are in no position to bargain for anything, except, perhaps, your old job back.

EVERYBODY CAN WIN

The old style of negotiating taught that someone had to win and someone had to lose. Women know that if you are a good negotiator, everyone can win.

Something that makes it possible to have a win-win negotiation is that people who are negotiating with each other often want different things. By giving the other party what *they* want, you don't necessarily have to give up what is important to you. For instance, when hiring a candidate, most companies want the following:

- **Best value.** Companies want the best candidate for the least money.
- **Salary equity.** Most companies have well thought-out salary structures that are benchmarked in their industries and are reluctant to hire someone in a position who does not fit into that structure or who is compensated significantly more than his or her peers.
- **No obvious discrepancies in the treatment of the new employee and existing employees.** Obvious perks that are uncommon for someone at that level, such as a company car or corner office, would create havoc in the ranks of the "have nots."

Before negotiating for any position, know what your priorities are and weigh them against what the company's objectives are likely to be.

Employees, on the other hand, are all motivated differently. For some, getting the salary locked in and having the cash flow is of utmost importance. For others, as long as the compensation is there, it can be deferred, such as in bonuses or stock options. For some people, albeit a smaller group, money is not the most important factor at all. For them, office space, project funding, or benefits — such as health care or vacation — outweigh salary in importance. Still others are motivated by titles and perks, such as health club or country club memberships.

Before negotiating for any position, know what your priorities are and weigh them against what the company's objectives are likely to be. Be sensitive to the fact that salary structures do exist and that you should not look to others like you got a better "deal" than they did. If you do happen to get compensation or perks that are better than those of your colleagues at your level, make certain that you never let on that your package was any different from theirs. The havoc you would wreak if you did this would not be career-enhancing, to say the least.

Other things that are up for negotiation when changing jobs are signing bonuses, relocation expenses, and mortgage loans. If something is important to you, don't hesitate to ask, but if the company balks, be willing to go to the next priority on your list. When you have negotiated your final package, get every aspect of it in writing. If the company is sincere in meeting its commitments, it will not have any problem putting it in writing. Make sure the salary, grade, title, and job, as well as the perks and benefits, are all spelled out. This is important not necessarily because you can't trust your hiring manager, but because others, like human resources or your boss' boss, often get to vote on some of these things, and you want to ensure that everything has been approved internally before you accept an offer.

Remember that nearly everything having to do with perks, salary, title, and benefits is up for negotiation; and your negotiating position is determined by your value to the company. If you are in a lower-level position and are relatively unknown, you will not have the negotiating power that you would if you were in a higher position or had unique skills that are needed. If you do not feel that you know how to negotiate for something you want, or feel that you are a poor negotiator, take a seminar or course, or read one of any number of books on this subject until you feel confident in your negotiating skills. Roger Dawson is one of my favorite authors of negotiating texts. Most of his material is on audiocassettes, also.

Every negotiation should be approached with the attitude that the end result can be win-win. A positive attitude and confidence that you know how to negotiate will help you achieve a balanced result.

Chapter Thirteen

Humor

*There's nothing more tedious than
a person who takes himself too seriously.*

-Roger Ailes

WHEN IT'S GOOD

Most top executives are perceived as having above average senses of humor. Taking your job seriously, but yourself lightly, is career-enhancing.

Some people do not believe that you can take your job seriously, and yourself lightly, but I believe that humor, when used appropriately, can enhance your career. It can make others feel good about working with you, it can change your own attitude about yourself, and it can break the ice in a tense or uncomfortable moment. Having a sense of humor at work doesn't mean that you are the office clown. It merely means that you are able to put things in perspective and laugh when laughter is appropriate.

In these times of corporate downsizing, restructuring, and reengineering, record numbers of people are being relieved of their jobs. The "survivors" suffer from overwork from picking up the slack, stress that they too may lose their jobs, and a sense of grief that they have lost their colleagues. Add to this the fact that salary gains today are not keeping up with productivity gains, and you create a pretty gloomy workplace where morale is at an all-time low in many companies. Humor, if used properly, can help pick things up around the office.

Robert Half International, a financial, accounting, and data processing resources firm, conducted a study of corporate vice presidents and personnel directors and found that 84% of them felt that employees with a sense of humor are better performers. Robert Half commented, "People with a sense of humor tend to be more creative, less rigid, and more willing to consider and embrace new ideas and methods. In today's business environment, if you haven't got a good sense of humor, the joke could be on you." In the same study, 32% of respondents felt that the people in top management had the best senses of humor. In a different, but similar study, Accountemps, an agency that specializes in placing accounting personnel, found that 91% of senior executives felt that a sense of humor was "important" and 45% felt that it was "very important." Primary reasons cited centered around humor relieving tension and stress in the work environment.

Humor at the office does not keep employees from being taken seriously, nor, if you look at the executive statistics, does it hold them back. What it does do is make them appear more human, more approachable, more likable, and more able to keep things in perspective. Even in the midst of a crisis, if you are able to laugh, it somehow makes things seem less overwhelming.

A positive and upbeat attitude aids the body in the healing process.

Humor in the workplace can be used in a number of constructive ways:

- **As a people-leveler.** When getting a group together for a planning session, brainstorming session, or any time you need creative input, humor can put the group at ease and allow people to feel free to create and innovate, unencumbered by rank or protocol. When the leader of the group exhibits an appreciation for humor, even if she herself is not funny, the group is more relaxed and comfortable and more forthcoming with ideas. Humor is also a good leveler in interviews or meetings when certain attendees may be tense or uncomfortable due to the rank or status of others in the meeting.
- **As an icebreaker.** Many people like to start speeches with humor because it loosens up the crowd and personalizes the speaker to the audience. Some people tell jokes, while others make light comments about things that have occurred at the conference or seminar the audience is attending. Either way, humor can be very effective at winning over a crowd, especially if it has been a long day and the audience is starting to tune out. Laughter will refocus attention on the speaker and will re-energize listeners after a long, dull day.
- **As a morale builder and people motivator.** People who are able to laugh at work are much more happy with their jobs and, therefore, much more productive. They look forward to going to work because they have a good time while they are there, even if they work hard. This attitude spills over into everything they do and will surely be noticed by your customers. Who wouldn't prefer to do business with someone pleasant and upbeat?
- **As a tension or stress reliever.** Humor can often be used to relieve a tense or uncomfortable moment. Often, when I have difficult news to deliver, I try to break the tension with humor. Usually the recipient of the news appreciates the re-

lease as much as I do. Additionally, when groups have been under stress for an extended period, such as when facing deadlines or working long hours, humor can help relieve the stress temporarily and revitalize the group. Humor is a good tension breaker in a group meeting when someone in the audience makes an offensive remark or asks an embarrassing question. By refocusing the audience on you, instead of the audience member, you are able to regain control and move off an uncomfortable topic.

- **As a teaching tool.** I still remember certain principles from my freshman chemistry class over 20 years ago because the professor was so good at making humorous analogies. If you can present facts in an amusing and unusual way, people will be more likely to remember them. Several months ago, I went to a two-day management meeting where the days were consumed with presentation after presentation of dry material presented in a humorless fashion. Finally, we had a speaker who presented his material in a creative and humorous way and recaptured the audience. It was the only presentation I remember, months later. Of all things, it was the financials!
- **As preventive medicine.** Many studies have been done about the negative effects of tension and stress on a person's health Other studies show how a positive and upbeat attitude effectively aids the body in the healing process. If you can use humor to relieve your own stress and keep your attitude positive, your body will be more adept at fighting off illness. It's both faster and cheaper than a doctor.

Even if your attempt at humor bombs, your attempt shows that you don't take yourself too seriously.

Some people are afraid to use humor because they are concerned that it will bomb. If it does, it does, but at least your attempt shows that you don't take yourself too seriously and can keep things in perspective. When you use planned humor, such as in a speech or presentation, practice it on a few others to ensure that it works, and have a good fall-back line if it doesn't. In her book, *Speak Like a Pro*, Maggie Bedrosian suggests two recovery lines often used by professionals:

- "What are you, an audience or an oil painting?"
- "So what is this, a staring ovation?"

If you watch late night television, you will pick up a number of recovery lines used by Jay Leno and David Letterman when their jokes fail to get the desired response. It happens to everyone, so don't panic.

Just be sure your choice of humor is appropriate and inoffensive. Ronald Reagan was a master at using humor in his speeches and presentations and effectively used it to allay concerns about his age in his re-election campaign when he ran against the much younger Walter Mondale. Knowing that he would certainly be asked a question about his age in the debate preceding the election, Reagan carefully rehearsed the line that brought down the house. When asked whether he felt age was an issue in the campaign, Reagan replied, "I refuse to make an issue of my opponent's youth and inexperience." The question was never asked again.

WHEN IT'S NOT SO GOOD

Humor is inappropriate if it is offensive or distracts from business.

There are times when humor should not be used, however. These times include:

- **When the audience may be offended.** This would include racial, ethnic, or sexual jokes or innuendoes. They are almost always inappropriate, regardless of your audience. Even if you think it's not offensive, the subject matter is too risky for today's politically sensitive audiences. Sometimes, humor that works with one audience falls flat with another because of their ethnic or gender differences, as demonstrated by this man's experience:

I was working in Saudi Arabia for a while. One of the cultural events that took place there every year was a desert picnic. I had never been to one before, so I was really put on the spot when our host asked each one of us to get up and tell a story or a joke. I was the first to speak, so I was very uncertain of what would be considered appropriate. Trying to come up with something on the fly, I ended up telling this story: "Three women found a magic lamp, and upon rubbing it, were granted one wish apiece by the lamp's genie. The first woman asked to be made twice as smart as she already was. This was granted. The second asked to be twice as smart as the first now was. This was granted. The third asked to be twice as smart as the second now was. The genie refused, and asked her to wish for something else. After much haggling, she insisted and finally, the genie relented. He turned her into a man." The all-male audience thought the joke was great, and I was relieved to be able to go back to my seat.

About a year later, I was back in the U.S. and was addressing my new staff, which was predominantly female. As an icebreaker, I decided to begin the meeting with a joke. Remembering how well the genie joke went over in Saudi Arabia, I decided to tell that one. I was shocked when I got to the punchline and nobody laughed. I don't know, maybe they would have laughed if the genie had turned a man into a woman.

Remember, just because one group is not offended doesn't mean another will not be.

- **When you risk hurting someone's feelings.** This would include remarks about someone's clothes, recent hair transplant, spouse, nose job, or other things of a personal nature that the person may be sensitive about. The following is a true example of a most inappropriate use of humor as told by one woman:

A few years back, I was engaged to be married in late summer. About 10 days before the scheduled wedding, my father died unexpectedly. Needless to say, we postponed the wedding. Knowing what our corporate policy was on bereavement, I was surprised that my boss did not send flowers to the funeral. Upon my return to the office, I was even more surprised to find that he had charged my leave against vacation, instead of the normal policy of charging it against bereavement leave.

These points of insensitivity poured salt in the wounds already created by my father's death and the last minute cancellation of our wedding. Over the next four months, I felt that my relationship with my boss was strained as a result of his actions.

That December, my fiancé and I attended my company's Christmas party. As we walked in the door, we encountered a group right in the middle of the floor that consisted of my boss, some of my peers, and several of the people who worked for me. I couldn't believe my ears when my boss gathered the group around and said he wanted to "make an announcement." His "announcement" consisted of a series of jokes about death and marriage and ended with a comment to my fiancé about how "lucky" he was to have been "rescued" from marriage by my father's death.

The group stood there in stunned silence. As what he had just said sunk in, I burst into tears. As anyone who has lost a loved one knows, the holidays are a particularly sensitive time anyway, and to have my grief made light of in public was more than I could bear. We turned and left the party. We'd been there less than 15 minutes. As we were leaving, you could hear my boss say, "What's the matter with her?"

- **When it is a reaction to something serious that someone is telling you.** People should never be made to feel that you did not take them seriously or ignored their feedback when they were trying to communicate something important to them. Regardless of how tempting it may be, it is inappropriate to respond with humor, especially if they are having a difficult time delivering their message.
- **When it gets the people involved off-track from the business at hand.** I have been in meetings where group members relentlessly made humorous, but distracting, comments that totally got us off the agenda and, in the end, were very disruptive. Humor should be used to augment the business, not distract from it. When it's used, it should be relevant to the business at hand.

I consider humor such an important balance to the seriousness of our business and so important to our mental health in the workplace, that when I interview candidates, I always look for a sense of humor and a quick wit. They are usually a sign of a keen intellect and a fast thinker. If the candidate is not humorous, then it is important that she at least be able to appreciate the humor of others. People who cannot laugh at work always concern me — I worry that they are too rigid and inflexible for our dynamic environment.

DIFFERENCES IN MEN'S AND WOMEN'S STYLES

Because of differences in men's and women's typical humor styles, it is best to use neutral humor when in a group.

Men and women tend to lean toward different types of humor. Women's humor tends to be self-deprecating, while men prefer teasing and mocking others. This presents a potential problem with interpretation. Men can interpret women's self-deprecating remarks as lack of self-confidence, and women can interpret men's teasing and mocking as hostile. When you are dealing with a mixed audience, it is important to note this potential for misinterpretation and strive for humor that is on neutral ground.

Neutral humor includes amusing anecdotes, quotes from others, cartoons, or funny stories that are not racial, ethnic, or gender-related. It is all right to use *some* self-deprecating humor, as long as it is not used excessively. A little bit makes others think you are secure and have enough self-esteem to take yourself lightly. Too much makes others think you are insecure and neurotic. Again, as with most things in business, it's a delicate balancing act.

HOW TO IMPLEMENT HUMOR IN THE WORKPLACE

It is up to the manager to create an environment where humor can thrive.

For humor to be effective in your organization, you don't necessarily have to be funny. You just need to have a good sense of humor and appreciate fun and humor in others. To create an environment where humor can thrive:

- Use cartoons or comics in your presentations. Keep a humor file and cut out jokes and cartoons during the year. Drop them in the file as you find them, and when it's time to make a presentation, leaf through the file to pick out appropriate ones. There are many good sources for this — the *Wall Street Journal, The New Yorker, Reader's Digest*, and most airline magazines have anecdotes and cartoons sprinkled throughout.

- Have a humor bulletin board in the coffee or copy room where others can contribute their own humorous notes and quotes. Make sure you contribute to it occasionally.

- Start presentations or speeches with humor. Real-life anecdotes tailored to your audience are very effective. So are humorous quotes from others. These are far less risky than jokes.

- Give out humorous gifts at staff meetings or offsite business meetings to commemorate events like anniversaries, birthdays, sales, or other accomplishments.

- Dare to use humorous notes or quotes in your internal memos. Again, refer to your "humor" file.

- Spoof company traditions when it is appropriate. Intel publishes a spoof of its company newsletter each April Fool's day, primarily making fun of its officers and their trials and tribulations over the past year.

Use these ideas to put together your own "humor implementation plan," so you can start increasing the productivity of your own organization.

Chapter Fourteen

Derailers

*The moment you let avoiding failure become
your motivator, you're down the path of inactivity.
You can stumble only if you're moving.*

-Roberto Goizueta

CHOICES — CONSCIOUS AND UNCONSCIOUS

**Low self-esteem causes some women to doubt that they can handle
certain jobs for which they are eminently qualified or to take
risks that men would routinely take in their careers.**

Despite all the goal setting, career planning, and hard work, many
women find that their careers have been derailed. Sometimes this is
through conscious choice — women have opted to have children and
drop out of the work force for a while. Or they have decided to spend
more time with their children while they are working and to turn
down the high-risk, high-reward jobs that would get them to the top.

Sometimes women just decide that they are not willing to make the sacrifices that are required for some of the top jobs.

In a recent *USA Today* article, Linda Chavez, former Deputy Assistant to President Reagan, recalled how she made a conscious decision to turn down an ambassadorial appointment, even though she was intrigued by the job, because of the status of her family at the time. Her take on the glass ceiling is that climbing the corporate ladder "often entails cutthroat competition involving 80- and 90-hour work weeks, frequent moves and a fanatical devotion to the job above all else. Few women are willing to play by those rules for long."

Making conscious choices is a part of life, and something we must all live with. What is of more concern is how many women derail themselves unconsciously. Low self-esteem causes some women to doubt that they can handle certain jobs for which they are eminently qualified or to take risks that men would routinely take in their careers. Research shows that the self-esteem problem begins with most women when they are adolescents. Prior to puberty, there are no discernible differences between girls' and boys' math and science skills. Once the girls reach adolescence, the boys, on average, pull ahead in these subjects.

Socialization that may impact these girls' self-esteem may start early. According to *The Wall Street Journal*, a New Jersey kindergarten gives out different awards to boys and girls each year. The boys' awards include ones for:

- Very Best Thinker
- Most Eager Learner
- Most Scientific
- Best Sense of Humor

The girls' awards are of a different nature:

- All-Around Sweetheart
- Sweetest Personality

- Biggest Heart
- Best Helper

These children are learning, in their first exposure to organized education that boys and girls are measured differently. Will the girls grow up to believe that being the "Best Helper" is a better path to success than being the "Most Scientific?" If this is true, our educational system is setting a dangerous precedent.

Something must change in our educational system and the way we train our daughters to prevent them from derailing themselves because of their own lack of confidence in their abilities to take control.

Some schools, in an attempt to help with the self-esteem problem, are beginning to experiment with all-girl classes in math and the sciences with extraordinarily positive results. Early data would indicate that the girls in coed classes "take a dive" in these courses to keep from being ridiculed by their male counterparts — a problem not encountered in same-gender classes. Likewise, studies of all-female colleges and universities have shown that the graduates typically have higher self-esteem and more developed leadership skills than their counterparts from coed universities.

Critics of same-gender education claim that this creates an artificial environment for these women and ill prepares them for the reality of the male-dominated business world; however, the scores of highly successful women in business, academia, and politics who graduated from all-female colleges and universities would dispute this.

The recent invention of "Take Our Daughters to Work Day" was intended to give adolescent and preadolescent girls a glimpse at some different and nontraditional paths to which they could aspire in their careers. In an attempt at equity, some companies encouraged parents to bring sons as well as daughters. It was discovered, much to the parents' dismay at one auto manufacturer, that when the mixed group was allowed to tour the plant and play with the automotive simulator, the boys pushed the girls aside and took the controls away from them. Clearly, this was not a confidence-building experience for these young women; yet the girls allowed it to happen, the parents allowed it to happen, and so did the sponsoring company.

Will these same young women be socialized over the next 10 years so that when they descend on corporate America, they will still allow the men to push them aside and take the controls? Something must change in our educational system and the way we train our daughters to prevent them from derailing themselves because of their own lack of confidence. There are certainly enough external derailers facing all corporate executives without having to deal with internal ones as well.

BEHAVIORAL DERAILERS

In order to succeed, businesswomen must do more things right and fewer things wrong than their male counterparts.

Ann Morrison's book, *Breaking the Glass Ceiling*, stated that interviews and research show that in order to succeed, businesswomen must do more things right and fewer things wrong than their male counterparts. This supports the theory that there is indeed a narrow band of acceptability for women — so narrow that at times it seems like a tightrope. Some of the more common derailers in women's behavior include:

- **Being too political.** As mentioned in Chapter Six, being too political can be deadly for a woman's career. On the other hand, being too apolitical can completely stall anyone's ascension up the ladder. The trick is to be tuned in sufficiently with the corporation's politics to stay out of trouble but not so steeped in politics as to be branded "political." This is indeed a tightrope, and one from which you must not fall.

- **Not fitting in.** Remember, corporations all have a culture. The higher up the ladder you progress, the more you are expected to represent the corporation to others — both internally and externally. If you are too "counterculture," you will not be perceived as a viable candidate to represent the corporation. The good news for women in the current global environment is that most corporations now wish to be perceived as diverse and flexible — images that women strengthen.
- **Pushing too hard, wanting too much.** This is a major derailer for men and women alike. When employees are perceived as overly ambitious or overly concerned with perks or benefits not normally associated with their positions, the concern is that they are too self-serving and not sufficiently interested in the good of the corporation. Consider your decision if you are the executive charged with filling a key job and you have two qualified candidates — one who is perceived as dedicated, hard-working, and company oriented, and another who is self-serving and so intent on getting ahead that you question the person's motives and ethics. The choice becomes obvious.
- **Lacking trust or support in the organization.** Having internal support — of peers, bosses, and subordinates — is key to getting ahead. Having no support is key to getting derailed. Successful executives succeed by getting things done — most of which is accomplished by influencing others. Without an infrastructure or network of support, usually built on mutual trust and respect, most people will not be effective in the long run and their careers will stall.
- **Not performing.** As mentioned in Chapter Three, it is essential to perform in every assignment and in every job. If you have poor performance and do not correct it immediately, nothing can

keep you on the fast track. Make sure you have the training and support you need to be consistently successful.

- **Being negative**. People want to promote other people who believe in the company and its goals. If you are perceived as a negative person who finds fault with everything the company and everyone in it does, it will be hard to convince someone that he or she should make an investment in your career. It is essential to be a realist — see both the positive and negative in every situation — then play up the positive and minimize the negative. It's extraordinarily difficult to convince someone that you are a "can do" person if you whine and complain all the time.

Inability to adapt or deal with change is becoming a more common derailer in today's dynamic environment.

- **Inability to deal with change.** With all of the change in corporate America: restructuring, downsizing, and new bosses; corporations need executives who can deal with change and changing environments without coming apart at the seams and without losing focus on the business objectives. Inability to adapt to or deal with change is becoming a more common derailer in today's dynamic environment.
- **Lack of awareness.** Not being able to understand how employees, bosses, or peers view you, or how your business partners or clients view your company or products, is a major derailer for both male and female executives. Lack of self-awareness was a temporary derailer for Anne Busquet, a senior executive at American Express. She had no idea how intimidating her employees found her, or how frightening her intensity and high standards could be until she received feedback that made her revamp her management style. American Express did for Busquet what many companies now do for key employees — provide them with 360 degree feedback from employees, peers, clients, and bosses to

240

show them how they are viewed by others and to give them pointers on how to modify their styles.

The Center for Creative Leadership, Lawrence A. Pfaff and Associates, and many other consulting companies now provide this service to corporations. Additionally, many corporations develop their own in-house feedback mechanisms. Computer Sciences Corporation (CSC), a Fortune 500 professional services firm, has its own "Institute for Project Management and Development Assessment Center." CSC uses the center to develop and maintain its project management bench strength, as well as to provide employees specific, focused feedback on their project management performance as measured against the company's success model.

- **Not recognized for their performance.** Having been socialized to be "nice," modest, and unassuming, women usually have a hard time ensuring that they get credit for their accomplishments. This, however, is essential to getting ahead. There are things that women can do to promote themselves without appearing too brash or aggressive (also derailers). They include dropping facts in water cooler conversations, copying others on "FYI" memos regarding tasks your organization has performed, using "I" and "my" instead of "they" and "we" when discussing accomplishments of your organization, and writing input for a monthly status report or your own performance appraisal summarizing personal accomplishments as well as those of your group.
- **Crying at the office.** Because women have been socialized to believe that crying is acceptable — in fact, even healthy — we don't hesitate to cry at weddings, funerals, movies, or at events where we are emotionally moved. Crying at the office, however, is definitely not acceptable, for a number of reasons. First off, many men see crying as a weakness — women who cry at work can't "handle the job" or can't "take the stress." Most men do not see crying as a normal and natural release of emotions — including joy, sorrow, anger, or frustration; therefore, when women

cry at work, most men don't know what to make of it or how they should react. One man said when a woman cries at work, he's "not sure whether to hold her, ignore her, or just leave." When I asked that same man if he would feel more comfortable if a woman put her fist through the wall, he replied, "Oh, definitely!"

• **Overplayed strengths.** Often, early on in people's careers, they will develop a level of excellence in stand-alone jobs where they have been extremely resourceful on their own. They may have been given tremendously positive feedback on their performance and, as a result, have developed high standards, little tolerance for weakness in others, detachment from the group, and a lack of concrete team-building skills. Later, when these same people are expected to perform in jobs where they must delegate, gain success through others, and build teams, they try to rely on past successes and don't understand what they need to do differently to succeed in the new assignment. Be cognizant of the fact that what worked yesterday in the old assignment may not work in today's assignment.

• **Willingness to accept a broad range of assignments.** Executive success is an equation comprising: basic intelligence + operational competency + leadership skills + learning willingness + good politics. Four of the five parts of the equation can be enhanced by a diverse array of assignments. This diversity can be achieved by line to staff switches, leaps in job scope, startups, fix-its, turnarounds, and task forces. If you believe your career has stalled, examine your breadth of experience, as well as whether you've learned the unique learning experiences from each of your prior assignments. If you haven't had learning opportunities, or haven't learned the lessons from the ones you have had, your career is likely to stall.

One recruiter told me in exasperation how many women turn down new and exciting assignments because they don't want to learn new skills, leave their current jobs, or even increase their commutes. These are fine choices, as long as the women realize they could be career derailers and are willing to accept this as a consequence.

- **Fear of Success.** Many women, because of low self-esteem, or fear of being radical, being rejected, or looking foolish, derail themselves. They just don't see themselves as "being the boss" or being the one to influence large organizations or the entire company. They don't see themselves as *leaders.* For these women, I suggest that they take on smaller tasks at the outset and prove to themselves that they are capable. They can then "up the ante" and take on more complex tasks, building self-esteem along the way. They can develop the habit of taking risks and being successful, a little at a time.

CIRCUMSTANCES BEYOND YOUR CONTROL

Many thousands of people have survived their companies' being acquired by or merged with another. Many thousands of others have not.

Despite your best efforts, sometimes unforeseen events happen that derail your career:

- **Mergers and acquisitions.** Many thousands of people have survived their companies being acquired by or merged with another. Many thousands of others have not. If you are in a key position and your company is in the midst of a merger or acquisition, attempt to negotiate an employment contract with your current company that will protect your position for a period after the transaction. If you are unable to do so, request a meeting with the key managers in the other company. Express your desire to stay on board and contribute to the organization after the acquisition. Then hope for the best. If the acquiring company's strategy is to remove all the existing managers, there is little you can do about it.

In some acquiring companies, the strategy is to subordinate all the acquired managers under their own managers, essentially demoting them. If this happens to you, assess your situation carefully and determine if this demotion has indeed stalled your career or, if after an initial transition period, you can get back on track. If not, seriously consider moving on to another position or another company.

- **Reorganization/restructuring.** Many times companies will undergo radical reengineering or restructuring, eliminating many functions. If you are reorganized out of your job, look first for other internal opportunities. Be flexible and willing to deal with ambiguous job assignments for a while. Be willing to create your own job, if necessary. Try to make it a positive experience inside the company — a chance to do something different. If that's not possible, then once again dust off your resume, and put your energies into looking outside.

- **New boss.** Sometimes a new boss comes in who simply does not see the value in your contribution or your function. While you may not lose your job, you may lose your place on the fast track. Always schedule an "interview" with a new boss to talk about what you do and your qualifications for doing it. Sell a new boss on your value to the organization and solicit support for your personal goals and career plan. If the boss does not value you and the job you are doing or cannot support your career goals, have a frank conversation about moving to another organization inside the company that will be more supportive.

- **Fired.** With thousands of people being laid off in corporate downsizing these days, chances are you or someone you know will be impacted. New management could come in and "clean house" to make room for their own team. Lou Gerstner at IBM is a perfect example of this. Few at the upper ranks survived his hatchet, but that's understandable when he was charged with a major culture change and a quick turnaround. For whatever reason, if you find yourself fired, the important thing is not to grieve too long. Take a couple of weeks to get yourself back on your feet emotionally, if you need to, then make a job out of finding a job. Negotiate with your company for an office, telephone, and secretary to help in your job search and for possible outplacement support. Expect your job search to take one month for each ten thousand dollars of salary you are seeking (e.g., six months if you are asking $60,000). If outplacement support is not available, consider one of the many books on the market that deal with job searches. My personal favorite is *Rites of Passage* by John Lucht.

GETTING BACK ON TRACK

What separates successful people from those who don't reach top positions is how they deal with adversity. Successful people take every experience — positive and negative — and turn it into a learning and growing experience.

Most people in executive positions have had at least one major setback — many have been fired at one time or another. There's no way to prepare you for the shock and dismay at finding out that suddenly all bets are off and you have been derailed. What separates successful people from those who don't reach top positions is how they deal with this and other types of adversity. Successful people take every experience — positive and negative — and turn it into a learning and growing experience.

Getting derailed doesn't have to be permanent. Examine what happened, assess any changes you need to make in approach or style as a result, and get back on the horse. Women have an advantage here in bouncing back, because they are not afraid to ask for feedback or help in changing perceived weaknesses. Furthermore, women are adept at the art of compromise and are quick learners. Take advantage of these traits to get back on track.

Chapter Fifteen

Doing Your Own Thing

*Being in charge is a calling, and it takes
a kind of talent....Someone has to be the leader.
Someonehas to be slightly crazed, obsessive,
and willing to set a high standard.*

-Mary Baechler

WHY WOMEN GO INTO BUSINESS FOR THEMSELVES

**Forty-five percent of women ages 35 to 49 thought about starting
their own businesses last year. Today, one in every 10 workers in
the U.S. works for a woman-owned company.**

Many women have decided not to go the corporate route, but
instead to start their own businesses. From 1991 to 1994, the
number of women-owned businesses rose 42% and now account for
$1.38 trillion in annual sales. Women have been starting businesses
at twice the rate of men. In fact, woman-owned companies now hire
more workers in the U.S. than Fortune 500 companies do world-

wide. This is even more impressive when you realize that this means that one in every 10 workers in the U.S. now works for a woman-owned company.

Fortune magazine recently hired Yankelovich Partners to survey 300 career women, ages 35 to 49, about their thoughts at mid-life. Forty-five percent of the respondents had thought about starting their own companies in the past year. An astounding 48% of women, ages 40 to 44, said they had considered it. Imagine the impact on corporate America if all of these women left their current companies and suddenly went out on their own!

Women cite a variety of reasons for starting out on their own, including:

• Frustration with the glass ceiling in corporations
• A desire to add balance to their lives
• A desire to control their own destinies
• The financial rewards associated with being successful

All of these things are possible through business ownership, but at a price. Just as hard work, planning, smart decision-making, and just plain luck are key factors in succeeding in a Fortune 500 company, they are critical to small business owners.

In the throes of battling one's way up the corporate ladder, the vision of striking out on your own can be very enticing. To overcome the biases that block access to the top of the corporation, to have the flexibility to balance personal and career endeavors, to have control of one's destiny, and to make lots of money are powerful incentives for starting a business. From the experiences of the many small business owners I've talked to, I can verify that to some extent, all of this is possible through business ownership. When starting your own business, however, it's important to gauge the realities of business ownership and then to enter the world of ownership prepared to accomplish the goals you have set.

BEING AT THE TOP

There is no question that the title of CEO or president brings with it a level of credibility and authority that generates respect from employees, clients, and the business community.

Starting one's own company is a long-standing reaction to roadblocks encountered in trying to make it to the top of the corporate world. As the owner, you get the top position in the company. There is no question that the title of CEO or president brings with it a level of credibility and authority that generally extends beyond the company itself to the community in which the company operates. It opens doors and generates respect from employees, clients, and the business community. But does this mean that women business owners have beat the system and bypassed the biases that blocked achievement? Not necessarily. In trivial and important ways, the attitudes about women can still impact the woman business owner, as described by this female CEO.

> *Once when I was looking for new office space for my company, my realtor set up a meeting with the owner of a complex of buildings who had space to lease. I took my male facilities manager with me to the meeting. The building owner only looked at and spoke to my facilities manager. Despite initial introductions, this man, consciously or unconsciously, had decided that my employee was the person to sell. Of course, my realtor made several attempts to steer the owner toward paying attention to me, to no avail. Afterward, I gave the realtor the task of telling the building owner that he had lost the deal. The scenario provided many a chuckle among my management staff for a while, but, because I was the buyer in this circumstance, it had no lasting impact on the business.*

Unlike the example above, sometimes the impact of intentional or unintentional bias can have a devastating impact. Many women claim that banks and other lending institutions simply will not finance their ventures. One woman who tried to capitalize her fledgling business was told by the bank official that she couldn't have the money she was seeking because he was sure that she was "going to spend the money on jewelry." Even though women-owned businesses fail at a lesser rate than men-owned businesses, the banks do not necessarily recognize this in their transactions with women. A recent report sponsored by the National Foundation for Women Business Owners and Dun & Bradstreet Information Services said that of over 1,000 women business owners polled, two-thirds have had problems dealing with their financial institutions. An example of "trouble" is this: one woman who ran a financially successful business and made twice the salary of her husband was denied a loan unless her husband would cosign. In frustration, she took her business elsewhere.

The problem has become so severe that the Small Business Administration has intervened and started a pilot program to guarantee women entrepreneurs' loans before the women approach the lenders. Many women's business organizations have also stepped up to help their members obtain needed capital or secure loans.

BALANCING PERSONAL LIFE AND CAREER

Most new business owners find that they spend more time and energy on their ventures than they have on anything else they've ever done.

Many women see owning their own business as a way to achieve balance between their business and personal lives. They can set their own hours, perhaps choosing to work during hours that give them the most time with their families. Advances in information systems and communications technologies allow them to operate from almost any location — even their own homes. Many service businesses such as consulting, real estate, accounting, training, and some kinds of sales lend themselves to this kind of operation. It often provides great flexibility in that the owner controls the amount of effort needed by controlling the number of clients or assignments she accepts. Such arrangements provide fulfilling, lucrative careers for many.

For others, however, this kind of cottage industry isn't the answer. Many business owners need to employ more than a few people, have a specialized facility, higher financial goals, or just need to work away from home. These needs will limit the owner's flexibility to balance personal life and career, at least at the outset. Most new business owners find that they spend *more* time and energy on their ventures than they have on anything else they've ever done. In addition to long hours on the job, many find that business concerns follow them home and affect the quality of time they spend with their families. In fact, a significant reason many small business owners sell after the first year is burnout from the almost obsessive effort put into getting started.

One woman entrepreneur laments how women struggle to balance everything — even when they own the business:

> *There was a time when women who worked as homemakers had a position that consumed 100% of their time. Now, they work outside the home as well, so their total role is at least a 175% position — with their spouse or significant other picking up perhaps 25% of the slack. What did women bargain for? We clamored to work outside the home, not give up our parenting or home responsibilities. But we forgot to bargain for the equity in our relationships. When launching your own business, if you are married or in a live-in relationship, I believe it is critical to have spousal/significant other support. The financial and emotional changes are tremendous. One day you are*

on top of the world with a six-figure income, and then there are periods when you don't know what happened to your client base — in spite of your planning. There are controllables, and then there are uncontrollables that can shake your faith. Your support system is vital, especially in the beginning stages of your business.

CONTROLLING YOUR OWN DESTINY

To some extent, the small business owner has more bosses, with more conflicting direction, than most employees.

When you own your own company, you're in charge. You can control the major and minor decisions that drive the destiny of the company. You get to pick what the company does, how it does it, who is employed and how the employees are compensated, who the customer is, what firms will provide products and services to you, and how the profit is spent. This is tremendous power; however, there will always be real constraints on that power, as told by one business owner:

When you start a business, you think you are going to be free. Free from bosses, free from biases, free from other roadblocks that seem so obvious in a corporation. In fact, being in business can be a thousand times more constraining because the corporate environment presents one set of rules to live by. In your own business, you must interact with many different systems that help you interpret your future — the bank, your clients, your subcontractors, your vendors, your investors, and others. I believe it is possible to break the glass ceiling eventually, if you are successful at staying in business. In fact, I believe that all new businesses face similar challenges whether owned by

*men or women. The opportunities for women lie after the
initial startup stages.*

While the business owner doesn't have a boss in the traditional
sense, she is controlled by many factors and factions. To some extent, the small business owner has more bosses, with more conflicting direction, than most employees. Customers and competitors influence price and the nature of the product or service provided.
Employees influence compensation and the nature of the work environment. If the customer is the government, the government influences price, process, and profit; but for every business owner, the
government, through taxation and regulation, influences process and
profit. And, there is always the danger that the demands of the business itself will strongly influence the lifestyle and destiny of the owner,
as described by this woman:

> *When I began in the executive search consulting business
> eight years ago, I thought that after year one or two, things
> would get streamlined, and like any job that you have for
> more than a year or two, that there would be a comfort
> level and somewhat of a routine. Not so. There is a rou-
> tine to the execution or implementation of my service. I
> was, however, not mentally prepared for the change in the
> marketplace. The business climate is quite different now
> than it was in the late 80s. The Fortune 500 companies
> that were once my clients have juxtaposed with the under-
> $100 million firms that were once my source companies.*
>
> *This isn't bad, but it's not what I expected. Frankly, I en-
> joy the smaller companies, as they are more nimble and
> flexible, the energy is electric, and the opportunities for
> me and my successful candidates are immense. The most
> difficult part has been balancing marketing and fulfillment
> — the wrong mix can have you overcommitting or out of
> business. Also, coping with the more fragile marketplace
> has decision-makers taking much longer to make decisions,*

exercising a lot of caution, and requiring buy-in from several levels in the organization. This was not the case years ago.

A final note here has to do with the impact of being the top person in the company. One woman tells her story:

> *As a business owner, I was surprised to discover that I missed having peers in the company. In talking to other CEOs, I discovered that many found that it was sometimes a lonely position. Gone is the ability to grouse with peers over the state of the business, personal worries about the business, and "dumb" management decisions. With the position comes a required posture of strength and wisdom. Especially in small companies, everyone watches the CEO as the litmus test for company status. I found that if I sounded tired on the phone, my competitors, creditors, customers, and staff began to worry that things weren't going well. Likewise, when I was up, everyone felt good, except my competitors, who worried.*

Another woman says this, about being lonely at the top, *"Isolation is at times problematic and at other times a blessing. Confiding in a professional colleague that you can trust helps during trying times."*

In addition to seeking each other out for "affiliate" relationships and support, many small business owners are now joining CEO clubs and other organizations to provide a safe place to "let their hair down."

MAKING MONEY

Folklore and real facts support the notion that "doing your own thing" can lead to financial reward. Most interesting are the major success stories of people who have left large corporations and made it big on their own. A well-known example is Ross Perot, who left IBM to found the very successful EDS — and subsequently left General Motors, after it acquired EDS, to found Perot Systems. Like they were for Perot, personal financial rewards can be great for the entrepreneur if her company does well.

The key factors for success of small companies are not very different from those for large, established firms — good planning, adequate financing, first class service, favorable market conditions, and good luck.

Not everyone will do as well as Ross Perot. Having always worked for large companies, I believed at one point that I could make a lot more money in a smaller firm. I actively interviewed CEOs of 30 of the fastest growing high tech firms in my area and found that I made more than nearly every one of them. If money is your primary motivator, check it out with owners of companies similar to the one you would like to start before taking the plunge. You might be surprised.

On the other hand, many people start their own businesses, pay themselves adequately but not wonderfully, but then make a fortune on the back end by selling the business or going public. Once again, these are choices, based on where you are financially and what sacrifices, if any, you are willing to make.

What makes a small company successful? The key factors for success of small companies are not very different from those for large, established firms — good planning, adequate financing, first class service, favorable market conditions, and good luck. One could say that the last two of these are largely out of the control of the entrepreneur; however, luck and market conditions often boil down to timing, and the timing for starting and leaving a business or for introducing a new product or service is in the control of the entrepreneur. One female business owner said she believes the old adage applies, "The harder I work, the luckier I get!"

GETTING STARTED

Make sure you plan a way to procure flexible services as you are establishing your business, so that the infrastructure can ebb and flow with the business.

Despite the cautions mentioned above, business ownership can be an exciting, rewarding experience. Managing the constraints of owning your own business is part of the challenge. One of the most important first steps is establishing goals for the business. A great way to do this borrows from business reengineering methodology. It involves creating a vision of what you want the business to be in five years. This vision will drive the decisions you make now. An important part of the vision for the company over the long haul is how you want to end your participation. Is the goal to sell and move on in five, 10 or 15 years? Do you want to take the company public and stay on? Do you want a "family" business to hand down to your children? Knowing where you want to end up will help you plan your beginning.

Business visioning is a useful tool in the planning and execution of the business. For example, it can even impact how you pick an accountant. If the goal is to sell or go public, selecting a major accounting firm to review the company's financials on a periodic basis is a good idea. Even though these firms may be prohibitively expensive and not as responsive to the day-to-day concerns of a small business, a track record of outside reviews by a large, well-known firm establishes the credibility of the company's financial records that will be attractive to buyers. Many small firms with these goals will select a small, less expensive accounting firm to assist them throughout the year and bring in the large firm to perform annual reviews or audits.

Balancing the infrastructure you need to build with the revenue you have to support it will determine how quickly you will become profitable, as well as what kind of cash flow you can expect. Few small companies can afford a full-time infrastructure. Most will try to hire part-time workers or consultants for payroll, benefits, accounting, marketing, and even administrative or secretarial services. While you don't want to build an infrastructure you cannot afford, neither do you want to overrun the infrastructure you have when the company is in growth mode. Make sure you plan a way to procure flexible services as you are establishing your business, so that the infrastructure can ebb and flow with the business.

As the business grows, the business owner is faced with decisions about how to go forward:

> *As you become successful, it is a bit of a push-pull to stay small, if that is your choice. Other firms would like you to merge, sell, join them, etc. Give this serious thought. If your big reason for having your own firm was to control your own destiny, then to change size and scope would be drastic. If it is the isolation that is bothersome, join more business groups and other professional organizations. The grass isn't always greener when joining another firm. Having to account to partners after you've been flying solo can be quite an adjustment.*

GETTING HELP

A common pitfall of new business owners is the belief that they can and must do it all themselves.

Ownership can sometimes seem like a frightening proposition. With the independence of day-to-day control comes the responsibility to make sure that all decisions are made and actions are taken to ensure the health of the business and its employees. This can be a daunting responsibility for the new business owner who must combine executive decision making with the day-to-day operational tasks

Because of the deluge of activities required of the business owner, an important start-up activity is an analysis of what actually has to be done and how much of that should be done personally by the owner. A common pitfall of new business owners is the belief that they can and must do it all themselves. An honest self-evaluation of what you can and cannot do is critical. If there's something you don't understand or don't have time for, admit it and get help. One business owner gives this advice:

> *Don't spend time doing administrative or clerical tasks that hiring someone for $10 per hour could accomplish. Sure, you have to train them, but why sacrifice an opportunity to bill out at $100+ per hour? Give up the tedious $10 tasks. We always think we are the only ones who could possibly know how we want to have things done — this is not necessarily financially prudent.*

In the throes of startup, when finances are tight and time is at a premium, it can be difficult to find and afford outside help. On top of this, ego and fear of outside control may get in the way of asking for or accepting outside help. This is one area where women may more naturally excel, as they have been socialized to believe that it is acceptable behavior to admit when you don't know something. One woman sums this up:

> *Asking for help is not an admission of failure. Not to seek help with a problem is a death wish. We always think our problems are unique and worse than everyone else's. Not true. People are more than willing to give advice and even to sit on your board for free. Give something back to their business in return. Let one of their contacts intern for a few months, or support one of their special business or community projects. Bartering for advice is expensive only in time and can do wonders in building a long-term relationship.*

Be willing to hire consultants periodically for outside help, or even call on members of your board of directors for help in their areas of expertise. Many small companies do not have outside directors, but it is certainly something worth considering for another perspective on the business, as well as expertise in areas where you may not personally possess it.

Chapter Sixteen

A Call to Action

Knowledge must come through action.

-Sophocles

I believe a book is worth reading only if I am enriched or ener-
gized as a result. I hope that as a reader of *Chances & Choices*, you
will think or behave differently in some positive ways as a result of
what you've read.

For women, I hope I've instilled a feeling that opportunity is out
there for those of you who wish to take advantage of it. I hope that
the guidelines I've given will help you to think through the choices
you have, the trade-offs you must make, and the actions you must
take to further your career. If you remember only a few things from
this book, I hope you remember that:

- Because of changing demographics and the shift in our
  economy, you have an opportunity you've never had before
  to lead in our nation's organizations.
- The choices you make — conscious and unconscious — determine how far and how fast you will progress up the career

ladder. You should be proactive about weighing the choices and the associated costs, and make conscious decisions about where you want to take your career.

- In order to maximize your potential, you must be an obsessive goal setter and have an *intensity of purpose* in reaching those goals.
- As a woman, you need to work hard (and smart) to fit into the culture in your company and to make others comfortable working with you.
- Image is extremely important in the office and at the client site. For women, there is a *narrow band of acceptability* with respect to image and behavior, and you should be cognizant of the boundaries in your environment.
- You will need to develop skills in managing, networking, communicating, negotiating, and using humor in order to maximize your career.
- The worst derailer for women is low self-esteem. You need to control how you interpret outside messages that erode your confidence and self-esteem.
- In the game of life, we are our own umpires. No one else can tell us we've struck out. It's up to each one of us to decide what we want and to go for it with all we've got. Do not become discouraged or stop before you reach your goal. Do not let others tell you what you can or cannot accomplish.

For the men who read this book, my desire is that I've helped them understand some of the challenges the women with whom they work face, and how they can help the women get past those challenges. I hope also that I've raised the awareness level of some men with respect to how certain behaviors can hurt women and hold them back. "Nuggets" I hope men walk away with include:

- Women have many unique strengths to bring to our nation's businesses and ought to be allowed to fully contribute.

- Diversity has a positive impact on a company's bottom line. Willingness to employ a diverse work force can cause as much as a 10% per year difference in a company's return on investment.
- Most women do not leave companies to take care of their children. They leave companies because they believe their opportunities are blocked or limited, or they leave because they can no longer tolerate a culture that is "female-unfriendly."
- Women need male mentors as well as female mentors.
- Men have the right to expect women to set clear standards of behavior that they consider acceptable and never to waver from those standards.

The biggest challenge in today's knowledge-based companies is to learn how to capitalize on human assets. By recognizing women as a key asset and providing them with helpful, supportive environments and equal opportunities, companies, and, in the end, shareholders, will benefit. At the same time, women need to decide what they want from their careers, set goals, chart a course of action, perfect skills, and seize the opportunities their companies provide.

As you, women and men, confront the challenges of our competitive and dynamically changing business environments, heed this call to maximize the potential of the fastest growing sector of our work force today — *women.*

References

Baechler, Mary. "Loves Me, Loves Me Not." *Inc.*, September 1995.

Beck, Nuala. *Shifting Gears.* HarperCollins, 1995.

"The Boss From Hell." *Industry Week*, September 4, 1995.

Caudron, Shari. "Fighting the Enemy Within." *Industry Week*, September 4, 1995.

Champy, James. *Reengineering Management.* HarperCollins, 1995.

Champy, James and Hammer, Michael. *Reengineering the Corporation.* HarperCollins, 1993.

Dawson, Roger. *The Secrets of Power Negotiating.* Nightingale Conant, 1993.

Gray, John. *Men are From Mars, Women are From Venus.* HarperCollins, 1992.

Deloitte & Touche. *The Initiative for the Advancement of Women.* 1994.

Gray, John. *Men are From Mars, Women are From Venus.* HarperCollins, 1992.

Gray, John. *What Your Mother Couldn't Tell You and Your Father Didn't Know.* HarperCollins, 1994.

Heidrick and Struggles. *The Corporate Woman Officer.* 1986.

Heidrick and Struggles. *The New Diversity: Women and Minorities on Corporate Boards.* 1993.

Kroeger, Otto and Thuesen, Janet M. *Type Talk at Work.* Delacorte Press, 1992.

References

Moir, Ann and Jessel, David. *Brain Sex.* Carol Publishing Group, 1991.

Morris, Betsy. "Executive Women Confront Midlife Crisis." *Fortune*, September 18, 1995.

Morrison, White, and Velsor, and the Center for Creative Leadership. *Breaking the Glass Ceiling.* Addison Wesley, 1992.

Murray, Margo. *Beyond the Myths and Magic of Mentoring.* Jossey Bass Publishing, 1991.

"New Woman and NAFE Announce Results of the 1992 New Business Contest Survey: Women Tell Why They Want to be Their Own Boss." *New Woman Magazine* and The National Association for Female Executives, October 8, 1992, press release.

Peters, Tom. *The Tom Peters Seminar. Crazy Times Call For Crazy Organizations.* Random House, 1994.

Ravitch, Diane. "Things Go Better in Single Sex Schools." *The Washington Post,* August 31, 1995.

Reitman, Thomas, Milbank, and Solis. "Women in Business: A Global Report Card." *The Wall Street Journal*, July 26, 1995.

Rosener, Judy B. *America's Competitive Secret: Utilizing Women as a Management Strategy.* Oxford, 1995.

Schwartz, Felice. "Management Women and the New Facts of Life." *Harvard Business Review*, January-February, 1989.

Schwartz, Felice. "Women as a Business Imperative." *Harvard Business Review*, March-April, 1992.

Spinner, Jackie. "Women Do Well in Business, but Not as Well at the Bank." *The Washington Post*, July 27, 1995.

Stern, Paul G. and Shachtman, Tom. *Straight to the Top.* Warner Books, 1990.

Tannen, Deborah. *Talking 9 to 5.* Morrow, 1994.

Tannen, Deborah. *You Just Don't Understand.* Ballentine Books, 1990.

Walbert, Laura. "Uncommon Women." *CFO Magazine*, August 1995.

Walsh, Elsa. "Beating the System." *The Washington Post Magazine*, July 23, 1995.

Weiner, Edith and Brown, Arnold. *Office Biology.* Master Media, 1993.

To order additional copies of

Chances & Choices: How Women Can Succeed in Today's Knowledge-Based Businesses

- Send check or money order for $25, plus $4 shipping and handling to:

  BookCrafters Order Department
  615 E. Industrial Drive
  Chelsea, MI 48118

  (Please note the book title and
  your return address on your check.)

- Or for credit card purchases:

  Call 1-800-879-4214.
  (Orders only, please.)

- For inquiries or personalized copies, call or fax EBW Press at (703) 319-9631.